THE RITES AND WRONGS OF LITURGY

The Rites and Wrongs of Liturgy

Why Good Liturgy Matters

Thomas O'Loughlin

LITURGICAL PRESS
Collegeville, Minnesota

www.litpress.org

1   2   3   4   5   6   7   8   9

Library of Congress Cataloging-in-Publication Data

Names: O'Loughlin, Thomas, author.
Title: The rites and wrongs of liturgy : why good liturgy matters / Thomas O'Loughlin.
Description: Collegeville, Minnesota : Liturgical Press, 2018. | Includes bibliographical references.
Identifiers: LCCN 2018009877 (print) | LCCN 2017050487 (ebook) | ISBN 9780814645888 (ebook) | ISBN 9780814645635
Subjects: LCSH: Liturgics. | Rites and ceremonies. | Public worship.
Classification: LCC BV176.3 (print) | LCC BV176.3 .O46 2018 (ebook) | DDC 264—dc23
LC record available at https://lccn.loc.gov/2018009877

For Mary Paul Clarke, OSC
—in gratitude for all her support

Contents

Preface

"What's worth doing, is worth doing well!" is a maxim that has rung in my ears since my childhood, and we all know that it's true! Yet, when it comes to celebrating the liturgy, doing it well can be very difficult. Even when a great deal of effort has been expended, it may still not achieve the ends we as disciples desire. Over the centuries many have pondered what constitutes the criterion of what we should do when we celebrate. For many Catholics, this has been scrupulous observance of the laws; for many Protestants, what was warranted or enjoined by the Bible. Both assumed that a good liturgy was a function of the appropriate authority: if the authority mandated it, then that will work! In the mid-twentieth century, faced with the obvious faults of their inherited liturgies, churches sought renewal and reform and often in the process invoked antiquity as the criterion: if it worked in that pristine moment, then it should be good for us now. This little book takes a different approach—one borrowed from the world of architecture and design—and suggests that we use a set of interlocking principles as a way to evaluate what we are doing now and what we might do in our unending task of renewing the liturgy so that it may be a fitting celebration of our discipleship, a proclamation of the Gospel, and a living fountain from which we draw life.

As this book begins its public career I want to thank all those groups of Christians who have invited me to speak to them about liturgy, with whom I have run workshops on various aspects of our celebration, from whom I have learned so much, and with whom I have shared the Lord's loaf, cup, and love.

T.O'L
Nottingham
Ascension Day 2017

1

Why Is Good Liturgy Important?

The waitress came with the coffee, placed one cup in front of each of us, and inquired if there was anything else we needed. We shook our heads, and she finished her task with a smile saying: "Enjoy!"

This tiny incident lasted less than a minute and was in no way special. Goodness knows how many times I have been part of such a scene, but the interesting thing is that you, beginning to read a book on liturgy, are probably just as familiar with the scene as I am. The reason both of us can relate to this incident is that it is a perfect instance of how ritual impinges on us and is an everyday part of life. We tend to think that ritual is elaborate, arcane, and clearly marked off from the rest of experience. It comes with its own sights and sounds such as gorgeous vestments and ringing bells; it has its own soundtrack, probably played on an organ, and even its own smells with clouds of incense. It is far from the everyday practical, real life. Indeed, we sometimes use the word *ritual* to indicate mere play-acting: going through the motions without real sincerity as in the cry, "He was not really sorry; he just went through the ritual."

Like it or not, however, ritual is virtually always present when human beings interact with one another. Surprising as it may sound to many, it is terribly important to us, and when a ritual fails we sometimes get very mad indeed! Likewise, we all like to do things well. It is actually very hard to set out to be deliberately and consistently negative and underperforming, so we like to do our rituals well. But discovering how to do a ritual well—especially rituals that are as multilayered in significance as the Christian liturgy—is not as easy as it sounds. That is why I have written this book, and probably why you are reading it.

Before we go any further, let's think about that moment in the restaurant. When I went with my friend into the café we both knew what was going to happen: we had done it before and we expected the pattern of events to repeat itself. We not only knew what we wanted—a cup of coffee—but we understood how to order it, whether one finds a seat and then orders or vice versa, that in this situation one sits down at a table, and we knew that we would have to wait for the coffee to be brewed and brought to us. This knowledge was not just common to the two of us—though it was a private cup of coffee and our conversation was both private and off the record—but was known to the staff and everyone else there. Someone who did not share all these expectations, who did not know the procedure, would be simply lost, and others in the café might consider that person a nuisance.

We went for coffee. That's what we said to each other, "OK, let's get some coffee," but was that the real reason we went there? Did we go for coffee together just to fulfill a biological need for regular hydration? Coffee is more than hydration! It is a social event, a bonding between people that they enjoy doing just for the sake of it. It is something we share, and we like to share with one another. We were saying to each other, without words, that we humans like relating to each other. Even if we are having a business meeting, we know that somehow life is more than that and that sharing a cup of coffee may be as close as we can get to saying to each other that life is larger than our jobs and much more complex.

Having coffee is a shorthand for all these things that are both important and taken for granted. We only know that they mean something if the pattern is interrupted; we would be suspicious of someone who would *not* be willing to have coffee with us. Now we are sitting waiting for the coffee to come and we engage in bits of conversation that mark a boundary separating this shared cup of coffee from the formal meeting we have just been to. We may return to "talking shop," but we won't do it at the coffee table the way we did it around the boardroom table. We know this is time just focused on us and who we are. If we do not know each other well, then we will talk about the big game last night, the game everyone knew was being played, or the weather. We are aware of the ambiance: a café must feel right and look right. We might drink a hot drink in any situation, but if we are "going for coffee" we expect the café to be laid out so that we can talk, with good chairs, and appropriate décor: it might have old coffee pots on shelves or pictures of an actual eighteenth-century coffeehouse on the walls. Having coffee is part of our culture; we sometimes even call it "café society." This is not only known to us but to every global coffee franchise. (Marketing experts are often more attuned to humans as ritual-using social animals than religious ministers!) Indeed, the actual cup of coffee can often be just an excuse for all that goes on when we say, "Let's meet for coffee!"

Then the waitress came with the coffee. This was much more than pressing a button on a vending machine. Human beings were interacting, but we did not know each other's names and we did not really have the opportunity to have elaborate introductions. She had many people to serve and we were sitting there wanting to chat, but could I act as if she were a robot? That would be barbaric. We humans have to relate to one another because we are basically decent toward one another and like to help and be helped. Being relational is hardwired into us. As a theist I believe the Creator is responsible for this, and thus we cannot just ignore one another, so we use ritual. The waitress checked out that we had what we needed to have a successful cup of coffee, we acknowledged that we were humans by smiling as we answered, and she brought this moment of human exchange to a conclusion with just a single word: "Enjoy." Technically, if you asked a grammarian, she had just used the imperative. "Enjoy!" is parallel to a "Halt" or "Stick up your hands," but we understood it to be a special word just for such a situation as having coffee.

That whole trip to the restaurant involved a set of shared expectations ("having coffee" would be a good idea that we would like and find useful). There was a task to be performed (going there, getting the coffee and drinking it). There were technical tasks (clean tables, have cups, make coffee, clear up afterward), and it all took place in a culture, with shared assumptions and understandings, and with many levels of interpersonal codes. This whole complex event was made simple because one of our everyday rituals is "having coffee." Indeed, we know these various parts of the ritual without ever thinking about them because if any of them failed we would know it, seek to put it right, and would remember it. If we went for coffee and the other person did not speak we would know that either something was wrong or that this would not be something we would do again. Likewise, if the seats were uncomfortable, or there was a smell of stale food or old cooking oil, or the décor was wrong, we might say, before ordering, "Let's try somewhere else." If the coffee was cold or had tasted wrong or the service was surly, we would have finished quickly and not returned there again. When the little ritual of having a cup of coffee with a friend has been done well, we simply know it but do not even alert ourselves to this fact. When something goes wrong with the ritual, we are very conscious of the fact and might locate all our misgivings on the liquid in the cup: "I've tasted better!" Likewise, if you are in the business of facilitating this ritual, then you take care that the ritual goes according to plan and fulfills people's expectations. You want the satisfaction that you are doing right and that everyone who comes to have coffee eventually goes away satisfied. But the ritual of coffee, though important, is relatively straightforward; the rituals of faith are far more complex, touch all sorts of deep emotions, are very idiosyncratic, and have to satisfy a dizzying range of criteria if they are to meet expectations.

So why is good liturgy important and why should we study it? We are creatures who relate to one another and who communicate with one another, and ritual is central to these human activities. Similarly, we want to carry out these encounters well, and we want them to succeed in fulfilling our highest expectations. So it is important for all who plan or take leadership roles in Christian rituals to ask themselves whether they are doing them well, what constitutes doing rituals well, and how can they be done better? Moreover, if people running a café ask how the "coffee experience" can be improved, then religious people—who make the bold claim that they act in the presence of the living God—should see doing it well as part of the honor of being a human being acting in that presence. When the memory of the dedication of the first Jerusalem temple was written up, for example, the writers showed the importance of what they were doing by listing the quantities of gold, silver, bronze, and jewels used, and how everything had been made as richly and beautifully as possible (1 Chr 22:14-16). This desire is still with us! This human desire to do well can manifest itself in our liturgy by

- how we set high goals for the way we relate as sisters and brothers in faith,
- how we remember the great acts of God,
- how we model our relationships on God's love for us now, and
- how we proclaim our hope in God's redeeming love in the future.

Good liturgy—and improving the way we celebrate—is a core activity. How we celebrate is not a fuddy-duddy issue for an elite few whose "thing" is liturgy. Why? Because we are all ritual beings.[1]

Experiencing Church

We can also list more specific reasons why Christians just cannot "let the liturgy happen" but must think about what is expected by people, how well we celebrate, and what the side effects are of poor ritual. Mention the words "Chris-

---

1. See Eric W. Rothenbuhler, *Ritual Communication: From Everyday Conversation to Mediated Ceremony* (Thousand Oaks, CA: Sage, 1998), on ritual in everyday human exchanges.

tianity," "Christian discipleship," or "church" to most people and they immediately think of a building, attending worship there, and the rituals that they could take part in. The most obvious way we experience the church is in the liturgy. This is often what people choose when they opt to identify publicly as practicing Christians, and it is often that which they move away from as they drift from corporate discipleship. Looking at the liturgy, we have to constantly keep in mind what people experienced when they formally interacted with the church as part of its liturgy. Was it an experience that they—usually without putting anything into words—found life-enhancing? Did they feel welcomed and valued or did they go away thinking that it was a little inner clique who puffed themselves up by making themselves an exclusive group? Did they feel that the group around them was an open or closed group? Did it seem to be a very smug group sitting on its laurels or a group that was alert and growing?

But there are even simpler questions. Was it all such a muddle that no one knew why they were there? They were just there because they had always been there, and no one could relate to what was happening? Did its concerns somehow overlap with my concerns? Or were they just fooling themselves? It is so easy to self-deceive in religion that we can become unaware of our blind spots. The simplest way this happens is when we confuse the emotion of *solemnity*, a very powerful emotion that can be easily manufactured, with *sanctity*, the still small voice of the Spirit that can be found in the simplest of situations. If we as the church want to make high claims for ourselves as "the Body of Christ" and the "sacrament of salvation," then we need to be careful that what people experience is something of God—of love and mercy and hope—not just a mash-up of an opera (whether well or poorly performed) and a military display voiced over in a fuzzy religious language. If we claim to be the Christ's witnesses (Acts 1:8), then people deserve a lot more from us than that!

But the liturgy is also where most people experience not only "the church" but also "being church." When we gather for liturgy we *are* the church gathered in God's presence, but does that come through to those making up the assembly? Do I feel that I am just a spectator; others are the actors? Did I appreciate that I was part of what was happening? It is all too easy for the experience to be one of accessing a commodity or of getting something done. "Being church" is about identity: my having a sense of who I am as one of the baptized. "Being church" is about relationships with the God who is rich in mercy and with others who form a redeemed people of sisters and brothers, and it is about hope and mission. God's love transforms situations and calls on us to be agents of love and hope. I should come away energized, ready for a challenge, and empowered. But if I leave the gathering feeling alienated ("They don't want the likes of me"), or come away thinking that God is vindictive or has turned away from me, or that I am of little or no importance in the scheme of things, then the Good News has not been celebrated.

While it is true that even in the most careful liturgy the people can go away with false impressions, the sad fact is that it is often the case that the silent body language of how we do liturgy sends out signals that are the very opposite to what we say in the words we use and what we profess in our creeds. The simple fact is this: many people reject the Gospel because they have felt rejected by the experience of worship. They have been alienated from the church because their experience of "church" has been so alienating.

Liturgy is there to tune us in to the real. Worship should alert us to what is going on in the depths of our lives, link us afresh in our relationships with other people in the community of faith, and open us to mystery. In a traditional society—traditional in the sense that the structures of living are handed on between generations—this is not a big issue. Each generation of old women praying and lighting candles in the church is followed by the next generation. In such cases it is only those who leave the society (usually through migration to a city) who face the option of "opting out." In a modern society, faith is an option; faith and worship call us to opt in. Contemporary urban Christians face a decision: Will we tune in to the message of the Gospel and then choose to make a commitment to belong? For us, both *believing* and *belonging* are invitations, not assumptions. This makes us different from most Christians down the centuries and so confronts leaders of liturgy with challenges hardly ever faced by ministers even a few decades ago. This puts a stress and importance on good liturgy that is quite new within our history. We are like those early followers of Jesus who used the *Didache*. Before each of us lie two roads—one toward life and the other toward death—and we have to make a decision.[2] Liturgy should help to affirm us in our decision to walk in the Way (see Acts 9:2), support us on the journey, and help make that journey a joyful one. If liturgy turns us off, or gives us a confused idea of the conversion called for by the Way, then worship has become self-destructive.

Growing in Faith

Faith in the Good News and belonging to the people of God are not static. Despite what lots of people think,

---

2. See Thomas O'Loughlin, *The Didache: A Window on the Earliest Christians* (Grand Rapids, MI: Baker Academic, 2010).

believing is not simply checking a box marked, "Do you accept?" Likewise, being part of a community is not the same as having the card that shows you are a member of the club. Growth in faith and belonging is growth in a relationship with God. It can become more intimate, more enriching, more demanding, and more rewarding. Alternatively, it can become a matter of convention or can wither and die completely, even when the person continues to perform all the demands with punctilious care. Good liturgy can feed this life of faith, renew it and deepen it, and most people whose own faith-journeys have grown deeper affirm that this has been sustained and supported—among many other ways—by the liturgy. "Faith grows when it is well expressed in celebration."[3] But, equally, people whose growth is fertilized by bad liturgy can have that growth stunted and can develop weird ideas, ones that are the opposite of the Gospel.

Our understanding of God is of a mystery that is totally generous, totally loving, and we pray, "Our desire to thank you is itself your gift." Most ancient peoples thought of the divine as a force whose anger could be bought-off by fixed patterns of gifts and sacrifices, and indeed whose favor could be purchased in the same way. They had made a simple, understandable anthropomorphism: they made God in their own image. They took the power-relationship between a despotic master and a servant/slave, then maximized it to a cosmic size and acted accordingly. This is still a potent understanding of "god"—both among those who reject the idea of God and belief *and* among those who believe and indeed invoke the name of Jesus. For this latter group, the Christian liturgy often became the currency with which they paid their

---

3. Bishops' Committee on the Liturgy, *Music in Catholic Worship* (Washington, DC: US Catholic Conference, 1972), 6.

dues to "god," and many practices such as having "Masses said," numbers of this and that, or fixed prayers/actions to obtain that effect actually stunted their growth beyond these false views of "god." Liturgy is important. Positively, it can open up mystery. Negatively, it can bolster the very ideas from which the Good News should liberate us. When the latter happens, not only is the liturgy a disservice to those whose growth is deformed, but since our liturgy serves as our shop window to those who are not yet disciples of Jesus, when they see what is offered, they can easily decide that it's not worth looking any further! Bad liturgy is a failure to witness to the Way revealed to us, and a betrayal of the command of mission to "[g]o, therefore, and make disciples of all nations" (Matt 28:19).

If we think about liturgy's importance in this way, then reflecting on what can make every one of us better "celebrants" of our liturgy takes on a new urgency. And we can appreciate afresh this little dictum:

> Good celebrations foster and nourish faith.
> Poor celebrations weaken and destroy it.[4]

---

4. Ibid. This statement has evolved in several other documents on the liturgy; see Thomas O'Loughlin, *Washing Feet: Imitating the Example of Jesus in the Liturgy Today* (Collegeville, MN: Liturgical Press 2015), 118, for details.

2

Ways of Assessing Liturgy

The incident lasted but a moment. A middle-aged man folded his arms, glanced around, and glanced down at his watch. Then all continued as before. The man was disengaged from what was going on around him and his momentary look at the time was a reaction: Will this last much longer? This was not the nervous looking at the clock we do when we are stuck in one place but know we must rush to another—like the way we keep checking the time when snarled in traffic, knowing that the flight won't wait—but the almost involuntary glance that is a visual sigh: How much longer do I have to sit here? We have all been in that situation. Indeed, most of us have been in it when at liturgy, and that glance at one's watch is, in fact, an act of assessment. Quite unconsciously that man had assessed the liturgy and decided that it was really not worth his while.

To many Christians the idea of assessing the liturgy seems strange. In the past, for most people the liturgy—

"going to church"—was just something people did. And today, for many who lead the liturgy, the notion that their performance would be assessed is frightening! But the fact is this: like it or not, we all assess what we are doing. There is a continual assessment process not only in every liturgy but in every group activity. That said, we usually only become aware of these assessments afterward. When things are going well, we just do them. If one is enjoying an evening with friends, one rarely stops and says, "This is a great party." One just gets on with it. The next day, if another friend asks what it was like we would rapidly form the judgment: "It was great, you really missed something!" We are a bit more reflective when our assessment is negative. We become aware that we are uncomfortable, we are annoyed with this or that, we feel irritated and we know it, we start being grumpy and in that state we can start listing all the shortcomings, or we can just feel bored: time is dragging. We also start thinking of alternatives. We notice that a moment is coming when we can skip off without being noticed. We start mental doodling: how many words can I make up out of the brand-name on the PA system, or we start planning what has to be done later, or wondering if we could just clear some email on our phones.

But if we are always assessing without noticing that that is what we are doing, there is also the formal evaluation that any significant action deserves. This is one of the reasons why we study liturgy. It is the reason why for centuries there were books on how to do liturgy and do it properly, and it is why churches need to be in a process of reflection on how they celebrate and why they need to keep reforming what they are doing. If good liturgy is important, then assessment of what we are doing—from the perspective of everyone involved—is part of the package.

How Did We Do?

To note that we are always forming judgments about our activities does not really take us very far. It is just a fact of life. Think of all the times you are asked to rate how some service you received was performed. How often has a question box popped up on your computer screen with a series of check boxes and the question, "How did we do?" In a hotel room there will be a questionnaire seeking your opinions and suggestions—along with a lure to get you to take the trouble to fill it in! Students are asked to give "feedback" on courses; there are even ways by which the notion of "rating your professor" can be turned into an offensive weapon. But while gathering similar feedback about liturgy might be an eye-opener for more than one minister, it is not really a way forward for our celebrations for several reasons. First and foremost, the question "How did we do?" is given by one group—let's call them "the providers"—to another group: "the users." This implies that "religion" or "liturgy" is a commodity that is provided as a service to be consumed. If that is the perception—and it is already one that is deeply set in the attitudes of many—then we have already lost! We assemble to celebrate, not to utilize a service. Second, liturgy is far more complex than anything that we can set out in a series of check boxes. We are involved emotionally, in terms of our memory and expectations, and it touches on our identity and hopes—that's why changes can provoke such outrage—and so we cannot just give it a score.

Moreover, we engage in it with our bodies and the way we do it is inscribed deeply in our memories. Liturgy is a way of behaving and far more than just a manipulation of ideas. We react to liturgy as part of our identity and if we break it into small questions, we get lost in details and miss the big picture, and liturgy is one of the ways we build the

big picture—our cosmos—in our lives. Anything that en-
dangers that process of cosmos-formation is working against
one of liturgy's fundamental dynamics. That was one of the
problems of the old rubrics approach. It became ever more
concerned with getting the details right, but the overall result
was a liturgy that was alienated from most of its participants.[1]
They knew the exact height every tree should be, but forgot
it was a wood! Check boxes are a way of losing the plot, and
we humans have a history of losing it in these matters—just
read Luke 11:42.

Thirdly, there are some things for which we should use
the check box approach, and if we keep it for such matters
(and use it) we might all be happier. For example: should
we move the time of a particular liturgy; should we produce
special sheets or use hymnals for some occasion; is there a
problem with the car parking? Collecting such information
not only allows us all to serve each other more effectively but
lets everyone know that they are not just there. But there
are other aspects of liturgy—such as its connection to our
inheritance—where collecting check box information may
only reveal poverty of understanding. Even worse, it can
be divisive. Any group asked whether there is "too much
music," "the right amount," or "too little music" will tend
to answer in terms of their own predispositions about music
or the benefits of a quick liturgy. The real question is how
music can contribute to our celebration of this event on this
day in our community's situation, and getting to that point
is far more challenging than a set of simple questions.

---

1. See Cyrille Vogel, "An Alienated Liturgy," *Concilium* 2, no.
8 (1972): 11–25; and Thomas O'Loughlin, "Building Community,
Celebrating Liturgy—the continuing challenge," *The Furrow* 67
(2016): 80–91.

The "How did we do?" approach does acknowledge that we are always assessing that which involves us, but may not be up to the challenges of liturgical participation. So, given that we do assess, the challenge is to harness this aspect of our humanity so that we can do things better. In the case of the liturgy this means an activity that brings us closer to one another, closer to Jesus who is our High Priest, allowing us to become more aware of who we are, enabling us to hear what God is saying in our lives, and opening us to sensing the presence of God.

Approaches and Criteria

But should we assess liturgy at all? Some would argue we should just be there and treat it as a moment that is outside our normal experience. There is certainly a tradition of taking this approach, and there are churches that openly adopt this stance because they view the liturgy as coming through the holy tradition—and so beyond any significant reforms or human criticisms. The liturgy, in this approach, is perfect. If you think there is a problem, then that's a problem within you as questioner! The liturgy belongs to heaven; human judgments belong to the earth. To assess it is arrogance bordering on blasphemy. The liturgy takes place within a sacred space, a precinct separated from the everyday, the ordinary, the mundane. There is a temple—the *fanum*—which belongs to the holy and another outside world of human action: the *profanum*. The boundaries of this other space can be marked by walls, or icons, or an unintelligible language, and in there the normal rules do not apply. It is worthwhile to think about this attitude as it can alert us to some basic issues within Christian liturgy.

At the heart of the Christian message is that God is the Creator of all. The universe is not to be divided into the holy and the unholy. Rather, we have to discover the mystery that is at the heart of the whole creation, that is at the heart of life, and that pervades the universe. This is, after all, why morality matters and is never just a secular matter. We encounter the holy here in the creation, in its wonder and beauty, and in the still small voice that speaks in every heart. A liturgy that stresses otherworldliness may be buying into a human tendency of dividing heaven/earth, god/matter, order/chaos, the holy/the unholy, but it is not one that takes full account of what distinguishes our faith in God, the Creator of all upon whom all depends for its very existence, from a more general religious belief that there is a supreme being. If one cannot encounter mystery in the ordinary, then anything one discovers in the extra-ordinary will be irrelevant to the rest of life. When Christians focus on the so-called supernatural, they forget that all nature comes from God and will only reach its fulfillment in its return to God and that liturgy is part of that great cosmic process.

An even more telling weakness of the notion that liturgy should be otherworldly comes from our belief that Jesus of Nazareth is the Anointed One. To declare that the Logos became flesh (John 1:14) is to declare that God has entered into the ordinary. Jesus celebrated in ordinary houses, ate with people, walked among us, shared our joys and sorrows, and died in the squalor of a crucifixion. If we declare that Jesus is God-with-us, Emmanuel (Matt 1:23), then liturgy is—and should be—as much a part of ordinary life as shopping, meeting with friends, having to get things done, caring for one another's needs, or having a party to celebrate our joys. Jesus not only showed us this in his actions, such as eating with Zacchaeus (Luke 19:1-10), but used the ordinary as the model of celebration in such stories as that of the lucky widow's party (Luke 15:8-9) or the welcoming feast for the prodigal son (Luke 15:11-32). When he gave a command that each should engage in liturgy toward one another, his example was not an arcane ritual (of which mystery religions then, as now, are full) but the utterly mundane, indeed servile, act of footwashing (John 13:3-15). It never gets more ordinary than that! Christian liturgy is taking its cue from the Christ when it is part of the everyday, helps us to encounter God in the midst of life, and is rooted in the experiences, joys, and sufferings of the everyday.

But if some have thought that liturgy is beyond evaluation, many more have sought to evaluate how we do celebrate against a set of criteria in the hope that those criteria would either prove that what they did was what should be done or that what they objected to in another's ritual was corrupt. Liturgy—which is that which can bring us together—is very often the field where we fight other battles by proxy! The most widespread, and long-lasting, approach is that of rubrics. The rubrical standard asks if the action has been performed in accordance with the rules that are found in the liturgical books. These instructions were, indeed are, printed in red (*rubrum* in Latin) and hence the term: *rubrics*. So if there is a rubric saying there shall be two candles, the approach is to say that if you have not two candles, then you have broken the rule. While if you have more than two candles, you have fulfilled that rule but perhaps broken another!

This approach, despite the enormous energy that has been invested in it over the centuries, suffers from some fundamental, and obvious, weaknesses. First, it is easy to get rules right and just follow them, but getting to the goal of why you are doing something is far more demanding. Any fool can just follow the "standard operating procedure" but leading a liturgy is a creative and artistic act and calls for a touch of genius. Second, because rules are viewed legally, the emphasis is on the necessary minimum, and this leads, not necessarily but inevitably, to minimalism. But liturgy by its very nature must belong to the effusive, and minimalism rapidly degenerates into external formalism (and boredom). In a culture where celebrating is a positive choice, such formalism is destructive of the community of faith. Thirdly, rubrics become a matter of things, and concern just the handful of people who were, in the old days, inside the altar rails who were thought of as "the ministers": the performers. But the liturgy is not what one group does for another group who are just there. It is the action of the whole people of God. We are all ministers to one another. Fourth, rules and practices are always changing, so some rules are observed long after they have become redundant, while other very important practices have emerged but are not covered by rubrics. For example, until 1969 the presider was instructed to take up any crumbs that were on a special cloth called the corporal. As a child I watched this each morning as the priest carefully scraped the corporal with the edge of the paten in a crisscross pattern for these crumbs. Why was he not more careful in the first place, I wondered, as it would save so much work! Even more amazingly, the altar bread he was using was specially made (unleavened and glazed so that it looked like plastic) to be crumb free! In fact, he was clearing crumbs from a thousand years earlier when the Latin rite still used a big leavened loaf.[2] Practice changed when unleavened bread was introduced, but the rubric remained—and was followed in detail despite being daft. Likewise, virtually every church now has an Advent wreath, and it is colorful, festive, and part of our common memory. But it only became common in the

2. Reginald Maxwell Woolley, *The Bread of the Eucharist* (London: A.R. Mowbray: London, 1913).

1970s, and it is nowhere mentioned in the rubrics. In short, a liturgy can get full marks for rubrics but leave the people of God unengaged while there are liturgies that really achieve their goal and are full of rubrical mistakes.

Another common way to assess liturgy is to ask if it is beautiful. We are aesthetic animals. We appreciate beauty, we are attracted to that which attracts us, and we implicitly make links between goodness, truth, and beauty. The aesthetic, therefore, would appear to be a useful guide to good liturgy. However, once one starts to apply the notion of the beautiful, one runs into problems. The hallmarks of beauty vary from culture to culture, age to age, and person to person. We all want the beautiful, but the exact constituents of this desire are as various as we are. How often has a community been torn asunder by a skilled musician or a musically sensitive leader who has a real sense of musical beauty—as recognized by those who have a thorough musical education—but where it just does not match the cultural setting? The liturgy is not the concert hall, nor a place where anyone should pursue beauty—in art or language or movement or whatever—but rather, where the people of God celebrate who they are in God's presence.

It is better to turn the issue of beauty on its head. Really good liturgy will have a beauty of its own. This beauty will be intrinsic to it even if the décor, the vestments, the musicians, and the dancers are all in "dreadfully bad taste," and this inner beauty will be attractive and will lead to a growth in faith. God is the ultimate beauty, and that which leads us as a pilgrim people toward God shares in the divine beauty. This beauty is drawn back from the goal of liturgy rather than being seen as an ingredient we can just add or ignore. We should avoid anything that we all agree is tatty, ugly, or mean. Yet if we chase after what one group considers beautiful, then we are apt to turn off just as many sisters and brothers as we attract.

A third criterion that is commonly used is that of historical precedent, and it takes different expressions in different churches. The basic idea is simple enough. If we can find this way of doing liturgy in what remains of the liturgy of the past—treated as an ideal—then this is what we should do now. For many of the churches of the Reformation this was the crucial test of what was acceptable practice when they came together. If it could be found in the Bible or the New Testament, then it was OK; if not, it was just a human invention and probably corrupt. But they forgot that Jesus came from a liturgy-rich environment in second-temple Judaism, and this was so much part of the life of his followers, that it barely got mentioned.

The key point to note here is that we only know about the past to the extent that it has left traces, and these are always less than the totality. They are often (even when we have liturgical books) little more than accidental survivals. A great liturgical experience is much more than can be captured in the formal texts. Others, such as the nineteenth-century instigators of the liturgical movement, thought that the ideal was the medieval monastic liturgy, but forgot that what they reconstructed was an ideal and that the liturgy of the nearby abbey might have been pretty run down! More importantly, they forgot that it was very different from what happened in the nearby chapel where ordinary women, men, and children assembled. More recently, many have tried to reconstruct an ideal liturgy from "the early church" and to judge liturgy by how close or distant it appears from that ideal. But there was never one, ideal, perfect, and standard liturgy.[3] Similarly, Catholics sometimes look at what happens in Rome and think:

3. See the warning in Paul F. Bradshaw, *Reconstructing Early Christian Worship* (London: S.P.C.K., 2009).

that is how it should be done, but forget that the local parish has very different needs and probably far fewer resources than a grand papal liturgy. It is well to recall that our earliest Christian references to the liturgy, in 1 Corinthians, are *criticisms* of the way they are celebrating. Paul thought they were doing liturgy badly! Looking back to the past is like looking into a great treasure trove of ideas we can take out and reuse (and we do this). Looking backwards can be a great way of understanding where we are and why we are where we are, but it is not an automatic route to a better future.

What worked in an ancient Mediterranean society may not be useful for today, what worked in a medieval monastery probably will not work with a gathering of families with children, and most of the New Testament was written for use *at* the liturgy rather than to prescribe a liturgical practice. We can learn from, and imitate, the past, but it is not our master. Christianity is a future-orientated religion and we seek to celebrate God's presence with us now.

Lastly, there is the most prevalent criterion for judging liturgy: the consumerist approach. This asks simply if it suits me. If not, I chuck it overboard as a waste of time. We should not fool ourselves into thinking that any one of us is entirely free of this approach. All of us have at some point or another made a liturgical option simply because this was the type of liturgy that suited us. Indeed, the oldest choice in liturgy, which is between those who want Spirit-filled spontaneity and those who want formulae hallowed by inherited authority—a chasm already visible in the first century in the *Didache*—tends to get followers based on their likes and dislikes.[4] More importantly, if our attitude to liturgy is that

---

4. See David Clark, "Order and Chaos in the *Didache*," *Journal of Pentecostal Theology* 25 (2016): 287–96.

of something we consume and use, then we have already got a blockage in our understanding of a loving Creator who calls us into a covenant—a loving relationship—with God. We do not consume such a relationship. And when such an attitude of getting something enters into religion (whether that be "Mass" or "grace" or "righteousness"), it is very often destructive of faith or productive of faith surrogates such as superstition (if you miss out on what you should have got, you're lost!) or idolatry ("I just love the Latin Mass and cannot stand guitars"). A useful corrective is this maxim: one loves God, one engages in liturgy. Just as we would not expect a marriage based on consumerism to last long, such an attitude toward liturgy is, in the long run, destructive of faith.

Secondly, liturgy is more than our likes: it involves our identity and it projects our vision of ourselves, others, and even of the nature of the universe. This not only involves thinking beyond my wants toward mutual responsibility and care, but invokes historical connectedness. Our memory and our sense of identity—who we are—are hardwired together.[5] If we forget that liturgy is always going to be tied down to that past (whether we call it the memory of Israel and God's great deeds or the memory of Jesus' triumph over death or the Scriptures or the tradition), then it is as if we could invent a new religion every time we meet. That said, whenever we meet, we are animated there and then by the Spirit, and so each gathering is always a new moment, a fresh start—but it is a new page in a long-standing love affair. Lastly, consumerism is fundamentally individualistic. That is fine if we each order from the counter our own food and then just

5. Paul Connerton, *How Societies Remember* (Cambridge: Cambridge University Press, 1989), 72–104.

happen to share the same hall while eating; but liturgy is a communal event, we do it together, and so if "what I like" is the fundamental criterion, many will feel alienated. We all know that when a presider at the liturgy decides that "what I like is what we will do" is the way forward, the community is sundered by others voting with their feet. The practice of every church needs to be diverse enough for many tastes to be satisfied, and the "what I want" approach is a tendency we need to keep in check.

The Principles of Good Design

There is another approach to finding out what is good: seeking out the common principles that might run through a wide variety of particular expressions, situations, and events. This way of promoting what is good (and identifying what is unsatisfactory) was put forward for designers/architects by Dieter Rams, a German designer, back in the 1970s.[6] He wanted to identify some elements that he found in every well-designed product, no matter how different the products or how varied the ways of approaching a design challenge. He said that every good design was (1) innovative, (2) making the product useful, (3) aesthetic, (4) making the product understandable, (5) unobtrusive, (6) honest, (7) long-lasting, (8) thorough to the last detail, (9) environmentally friendly, and that (10) "good design is as little design as possible."

There are two proofs that Rams was really onto something. First, if you look at the products that you and I choose over and over again—so that they become the standard preferences—you will find that they, silently, possess these

6. Just put "Dieter Rams" and "design principles" into a search engine and see the range of stuff that comes up!

qualities. Second, these principles have prompted many specialized applications for the good design of this or that, be that maps or computer programs or whatever. Now these principles cannot just be taken over into liturgy—they originated with someone designing material objects—but the approach of seeking our underlying common elements/principles has much to recommend it. Underlying principles work like a series of interlocking aims, and they are the opposite of a set of commandments or an in/out checklist. They work by helping us to see if we are going in the right direction. They are qualities we just somehow know we should be striving for, and sometimes we know, instinctively again, when we have failed to meet them.

So where are we? This book is based on the assumption that good liturgy builds faith and bad liturgy destroys it. The remainder of this book is an attempt to answer the challenge of identifying what might be the ten principles of good liturgy. Can we find ten elements common to liturgies that build the life of faith and whose absence means that a liturgy is failing in its ultimate purpose?

3

Principle I

Good Liturgy Is Honest

It was an old-fashioned church with fixed kneelers between long wooden benches making getting in and out, especially in coats, difficult. It was a special event with many visitors and one of the regulars did not like having to make room for them. Standing was awkward with knees bent by the seat's edge and toes under the kneeler. The presider called us "brothers and sisters" and said we were all *very* welcome—and then proceeded to bark out various instructions, culminating with this warning: "Jesus is really present in Holy Communion, so if you are in a state of mortal sin or are not a *Roman* Catholic, you must not take Communion, but if you come up and fold your arms [he showed the correct gesture] you can get a blessing." The physical discomfort of where I was standing seemed to jell with a feeling of emotional discomfort as I absorbed the presider's words and tone. It was not nice to be there. Just then, the guy next to me sighed and mumbled in a dull voice, "So we are all very welcome then."

The Human Value of Words and Gestures

Words and symbols are the currency between us as human beings. They pass to and fro, linking us, establishing relationships, and forming the building blocks of our worlds. They create trust, and upon their implied promises we set out to live our lives. When we think that words have become false or empty, we feel cheated. We feel we have to withdraw from those whose gestures and statements have deceived us. Then, with feelings of alienation we withdraw into isolation and, slowly, seek a new set of relationships in which we can trust the words and gestures once again. Whenever words and gestures have been proven false, we end up with a bitter taste in our mouths. Enough experiences of that sort and we can become permanently embittered and cynical and can develop "a hard skin" that cuts us off from those around us, making us suspicious, likely to see every gesture as a threat.

By contrast, encountering someone who is "the genuine article" is a moment of joy: it restores our faith in humanity and gives us, even in a bleak situation, a glimpse of the good. There is no wealth comparable to belonging to a circle of people, friends, we can trust. The truth of this is all around us: when trust breaks down in a society, the society itself breaks down. Homes become fortified strongpoints, we rely on blood-ties and family networks rather than on human fraternity, and "the stranger" becomes the threatening "other."

All moves toward reconciliation and peace, on the other hand, involve trust building, words having human meaning, and bridges building. The stories of Jesus in the gospels are those of a group that would stay with him and were heard within communities that were seeking to build just such communities themselves: hence their horror at the gesture of a betrayal with a kiss (Matt 26:48-49; Mark 14:44-45; Luke 22:47-48). Judas was not only untrustworthy as a friend (Matt

26:50; John 15:15), but even used fake gestures. In the early churches, moreover, they were well aware of the dangers of "prophets" who used the words and gestures of religion but whose real interest was personal advancement. They even had a name for them: *christmongers,* and developed a set of rules to protect communities from them.[1] In recent years the abuse cases involving clergy have been even more painful and bitter because there is the lurking awareness that these crimes came from those who used the language of trust, care, and love. Signs and symbols that have been compromised cannot be fixed like mending a broken washing machine: call the expert, get the job done. It takes decades for symbols to have their value restored and some are broken forever.

Because liturgy is a matter of language and gesture it is most sensitive to destruction by dishonesty. Hence honesty, a linking between what we say and what we do, is a fundamental quality both in the liturgy and between liturgy and life. Most people know that an alignment between what we profess in prayer and preaching and what we do is the very heart of the Christian vocation. We have the words of Paul in Romans 2:17-24 that are summarized as "practice what you preach." Within the actual liturgy there is an equal need for such alignment, so if we use words about what we are doing, they should be reflected in the way we act in the liturgy. If we use gestures in the liturgy and see those gestures as important, they should not be compromised by other activities nor contradicted by the overall pattern of behavior. All too easily a chasm can creep into liturgy whereby the words and

1. *Didache* 12:5; see Jonathan A. Draper, "Performing the Cosmic Mystery of the Church in the Communities of the Didache," in *The Open Mind: Essays in Honour of Christopher Rowland*, ed. J. Knight and K. Sullivan (London: Continuum, 2015).

gestures used at the formal level are negated by the signals that people are picking up in their actual experience.[2] When such a gap opens up, our liturgy is undermined and our ritual comes to be seen as the opposite of reality, as in the phrases: "It was only symbolic" (i.e., they did not mean it) or "It was mere ritual' (i.e., they were just doing what they had to, did not care, and their words were but empty words). This is a serious matter because honest words and gestures are so important to us as human beings that to have to live with empty words is a real impoverishment.

Some Cases

So what does the chasm within the liturgy between words/ gestures and our experience look like? These few examples may set in train an entire list from your own participation in worship.

We very frequently speak about the importance of listening to the word of the Lord but actually we make sure that the Liturgy of the Word is rushed through, and we fear moments of silence as if they were just delays. If we say that we want to have reflective listening, something that is a presupposition of many of the texts we read, then can we use means of singing the psalms other than full-congregation hymns? If listening to what the word says in each of the hearts of the baptized is important, then why do we jump straight into a mini-lecture homily rather than lead a time of mulling over what we have heard? To say "the word of the Lord" and instantly move on to something else just does not accord with the honor we claim such readings demand. The result

---

2. Thomas O'Loughlin, "Eucharistic Celebrations: The Chasm between Idea and Reality," *New Blackfriars* 91 (2010): 423–38.

is that we sense that we must say all this about the Liturgy of the Word, but it is not really that important.

Frequently in the liturgy we use the imagery of being gathered around the Lord's table, being guests at the banquet, or the imagery of the supper and guests, and we read umpteen stories of such banquets of welcome such as the parable of the Prodigal Son's return (Luke 15:23-24) or Jesus' eating at the table of the outcast Zacchaeus (Luke 19:5-7). It is a rich image with the deepest biblical memories, and it is a warm cross-cultural human image: the table and banquet are at the core of virtually every society. But using all this language, are we actually experiencing being around the Lord's table? Most western churches have gotten rid of the physical barriers between the table and guests (rails, grills, screens, distance), but for most, the experience is being in an auditorium, arranged as an audience, looking at a table with only one person, the presider, or a few special people *at* the table. Yet once a group has had the experience of being actually around the table, the first reaction is often an appreciation of commensality as both a human and Christian event, along with a new understanding of the Lord's banquet.

In a similar vein we use the language of being sisters and brothers. The clear implication is that we are all loved equally by our heavenly Father, and, indeed, the Eucharist is one of the earliest institutions where human equality was part of the package. The poor had to share with the rich; the rich were not to see themselves as superior to the poor or sinners or prostitutes. All were to receive welcome, even the Gentiles! It is a Gospel imperative that still challenges us.[3] But our liturgy

---

3. Thomas O'Loughlin, "Sharing Food and Breaking Boundaries: Reading of Acts 10–11:18 as a key to Luke's ecumenical agenda in Acts," *Transformation* 32 (2015): 27–37.

is often an exercise in separations, and when the chasm is experienced it appears that our liturgy is a deceit.

Why Is Liturgical Honesty Important?

Because we imagine our liturgy taking place, in the Christ, in the court of heaven (Heb 9:24), it is incumbent upon us to seek the greatest authenticity in what we do in a world of signs so that, at the very least, it is self-consistent and strives to be consistent with all that we preach. So, minimally, we should seek to remove dissonance between what we say and what we do. But the liturgy is frequently dissonant because it has layers of accretion that, unchecked, divert our sounds, actions, and theology. The result is a situation whereby it appears to be words—but words that mean little and can be seen as simply a clerical rigmarole devoid of genuine communication. There are so many examples of such dissonance in the contemporary Roman liturgy that I suspect it is one of the great, deep-level reforms that we have barely yet addressed. Consider the example of having a set of prayer texts (i.e., written texts) that proclaim the purpose of the Eucharist is thanksgiving to the Father in, through, and with the Christ—hence their designation: *eucharistic prayers*. Concomitantly we have a set of ritual texts (i.e., what is perceived by anyone present) that are focused on changing elements so as to confect the Christ's presence. What we actually hear depends on what we are hearing with just our ears or perceiving with all our senses. The problem gets greater when we seek to explain the texts—whichever we chose—to ourselves or to others (as in ecumenical discussions that, then, eventually end in all-around frustration). Consider the small details. We say, "Drink this," but then do not drink; we say, "He broke it," but use unbroken individual wafers. What we say and what we do in ritual do not come into alignment. Yet without this simple level of coherence, a coherence in the visible objects of our liturgy, we are called upon to assume that there is a coherence between the liturgy as such, our kerygma, and our own endeavors as disciples.

"Honesty Is the Best Policy"

If we are to avoid a chasm between the message that is the Gospel-in-celebration and the signals that are actually received, we need to keep our celebrations under constant review. It is so easy to utter words and make gestures but fail to see that all that happens at a liturgy is a gesture, a word, between human beings, and that word has to be worthy of its location in the divine presence. If honesty is a principle of good liturgy, then a transparent linkage between what is done formally and what is done informally, between what we say and what is heard, must be held up as one of our ideals: a goal toward which we should strive.

On the other hand, when the directness between our ritual words and actions breaks down—as it is both prone to do and as has happened during centuries of unreformed repetition—we end up with an infinite regress of signs: signs to signs to signs. This—as in all logically infinite series of this sort—eventuates as saying potentially everything and nothing. At best, we can hope to end up with ambiguities and, at worst, nonsense. A pursuit of honesty between the varieties of our signs must be a primary quality of liturgy. We might recall that it is precisely a dissonance between symbols and intentions that the Gospel narrator expects will cause shock in his audience at the event of the arrest of Jesus when a traitor uses a kiss as his identifying sign. In a word: good liturgy should do what it says and say what it does.

4

Principle II

Good Liturgy Is Joyful

The final words in the book had been uttered. It had been a very formal, rather long, and *very* wordy liturgy. Then the presider, sensing the heaviness of the whole affair, added a tiny ritual—not mentioned in any book or commented upon by any rubrician—looking directly at us, he gave a wry smile, and said: "Have a nice day!" That tiny human ritual changed how we felt at that moment, the spirit in which we left the building, and our remembered perception of our gathering.

There is a suspicion of joyful liturgy in many mainstream churches as if that is the characteristic of the worship of Evangelical and Pentecostal churches; in contrast, more serious churches do things in a serious, heavy, and dull way. Solemnity often takes the form of heavy structure, ponderous ceremonial, and elaborate grandeur. But while this may reflect a human sense of the important as the big and the bold, it may not be true to the smallness and intimacy of the incarnation, nor to our communal nature that loves parties!

All liturgy must somehow image the fact that Jesus was seen as announcing a joyful festival (Luke 4:17-19) and his disciples imagined not only their liturgy but their Way in terms of a feast.[1]

Most churches with a formal liturgy think that overt expressions of joyfulness are somehow a distraction from real liturgy or from prayerfulness. There seems to be an unwritten agreement that "happy clappy" is OK for those whose idea of worship is a "hymn sandwich," but not for those whose concern is with the breaking of the loaf! I once heard the suspicion summed up in this quip: "Pentecostals do emotion, we Catholics do *gravitas*!" But joyfulness means that we are not stuffy; we realize that only God is permanent and that even our most precious rituals are transitory: God alone abides! Faced with this, to take the forms of worship too seriously is a type of pious idolatry. Such idolatry is the worst case of confusing God with things because it all seems so pious to us. Moreover, to imagine that there is any liturgy that does not "do emotion" is an illusion *de facto*, while it also forgets the basic reality that we are emotional creatures and our emotions are part of who we are as we stand in the presence of God. Likewise, *gravitas* literally means heaviness, and sometimes we are bent double with the amount of heaviness in our lives. Praising *gravitas* can be a polite justification for being downright boring. Rather than fear emotion, we should ask what is the true emotional tone of a Christian assembly. A good candidate for that is one word: *joy*.

There are two real dangers that can beset the worship of churches with formal liturgies fixed in books. The first is that of confusing an *official* liturgy with an *officious* liturgy:

---

1. Michael Wolter, "Primitive Christianity as a Feast," in *Feasts and Festivals*, ed. C. Tuckett (Leuven: Peeters, 2009): 171–82.

where everything is done without any sense that God is loving and wants us to have happiness (see Luke 11:13) and so be able to be rejoicing and thankful from the whole of our being. The second danger is confusing *solemnity* with *sanctity*, forgetting that God can be found in all sorts of ways, must never be fitted into our boxes, or imagined as if God can be encountered only in prescribed ways (see Luke 18:14). Holiness is a transcendental; it goes beyond our plans and categories. We cannot assume that we have good liturgy because we have followed the program! And if there is no joy in it, it probably feels more like a duty or a debt rather than a response of love to love.

A Theology of Joy

Even in the depths of our sadness at a funeral, or of our recollection when recalling the passion of Jesus, we are a people of hope: the day of recalling the passion and death of Jesus is *Good* Friday. Our belief is in salvation, redemption, and the victory of love and life over death and dissolution. Any liturgy that does not manifest this is unworthy of being a product of our coming together in the presence of God. This means that our liturgies must reflect a tension inherent in Christian discipleship. We take all suffering most seriously, and we acknowledge openly loss and sadness—we die rather than *pass away*—but "our hope is rich in immortality." So even on the grimmest of occasions, we must remind ourselves of our joy. But, more commonly, in our day-to-day liturgy there needs to be the lightness and joyfulness of those whose religion is not that of a future of "the great crunch" but of the eschatological banquet.

An atheist philosopher is reported to have quipped that if Christians are redeemed, then their faces do not show it! Our response to this cannot be some sort of marketing ploy: the professional smiling, upbeat countenance of the salesperson who is "on message." Such a falsehood—and I have taken part in liturgies that were remorselessly upbeat!— is inappropriate when we are in the presence of God. But equally, the long faces and somber colors—common to the Puritan tradition and to much of the clerical tradition with its plain black cloth—is inappropriate. Our message is not one of doom. Death is a reality we face, not one that we must constantly dwell upon. In the aftermath of the Black Death in the fourteenth century—widely understood in terms of God's dispensing punishment—we overdid the notion of the *memento mori* and the attitude that anything but a dismal seriousness was vain buffoonery. We are redeemed. We may not always show it, but we can be joyful, and enjoying that joyfulness is part of our being children of the Father who loves us.

Anthropologists often note that religions are intrinsically optimistic. The raw fact of ritual proclaims that there is a future. Our good news allows us to go one step further. Joy has the last word. Therefore, we can express that in a playfulness and a lightheartedness. Life is serious *and* God is good.

But we can move deeper. Part of Christian wisdom down the centuries has been to acknowledge that our species is *homo ludens* (the laughing human); we are playful in our very core. We can laugh at situations, we can see the silliness of even the most momentous events, and when we gather, it is this playfulness that is at the core of our common narratives. Joy keeps us together, refreshes us, and allows us to set our problems in perspective. Joy refreshes us, and one of the roles of the liturgy is to be a refreshment for our spirits—precisely because the Holy Spirit is the giver of solace in woe, cool in heat, and refreshment in toil. We should always leave the assembly with a new pep in our step; we should have encountered joy there. If we believe that God has pitched his tent among us (John 1:14), then we should meet him elbow to elbow around the table. Should that not be joyful? If we, even in disasters, know that death does not have the last word in human existence, then a tone of joy in our liturgy is not simply a product of a vague optimism, but our manifestation that we are trying "to live by the Spirit" and to be "led by the Spirit" and so enjoy "the fruits of the Spirit" that are love, peace . . . and *joy* (Gal 5:16-23).

Joyfulness Is Always Unscripted

Rather than trying to build in joyfulness—as silly a task as trying to have a formula for happiness or genius—we can, first, remove dullness, that dark brooding seriousness; and, second, give ourselves permission to enjoy any gaiety that occurs spontaneously in the liturgy. This takes many forms. It means that there should be moments of real informality in every liturgy. Greetings and farewells should be unscripted in the same way that our everyday meetings with our friends are unscripted.[2] We should feel free to alter formulae found in liturgical books when the situation calls for it. Likewise, our whole style of presiding should have a lightness that conveys a sense that while this is not a game, neither is it a scientific formula demanding exact compliance. It also means that if someone is giving out notices and his only voice is that of a sergeant barking out orders, then maybe he needs to consider a change of ministry. Likewise, a preacher who is focusing on fear—fear of death, sin, or whatever—may not realize that

2. Thomas O'Loughlin, "Introducing a liturgy: reflecting on a moment of communication," *The Pastoral Review* 11, no. 4 (2015): 4–9.

he is, in his very demeanor, conveying a different image of God than that proclaimed by Jesus.

By contrast, when we hear calls for *gravitas*—as we do—we might ask these questions. Who mandated that *gravitas* is one of the characteristics of Christian worship? How often is it praised as a gift or fruit of the Spirit? And, could it be that *gravitas* is a camouflage for lack of energy, dull repetition, and a need to let everyone else see that the leaders of liturgy are very learned and very important people?

Joy and Abundance

If God is love (1 John 4:8, 16), then a true liturgy must reflect this, and joyfulness, a lightness of touch, a sense of generosity, and human warmth and welcome are its experiential reflections when we gather. John presented this link in his proclamation in the story of Cana in Galilee (2:1-11). A gathering of the people of God, celebrating the archetypal ritual of joy, a wedding, encounter an unplanned situation that would rob the event of an essential ingredient for it to be a moment of community joyfulness, full of spontaneity: the wine ran out! Jesus is called upon in this embarrassing and distressful situation and he manifests his glory by gently restoring joy and calm. But what a restoration! Six stone jars "each holding twenty or thirty gallons." Anyone who has seen these stone vessels—they were favored by the Pharisees because, unlike pottery, they could not become ritually impure—knows that they are never very large, usually only capable of holding a couple of pints, and certainly not "twenty or thirty gallons"! And we can be sure of this: with all that wine, *gravitas* would not be the hallmark of the event that is presented by John as the first manifestation of Jesus' glory! So why the hyperbole in the preaching? The notion of a feast with between 120 and 180 gallons of very good wine is a way of conveying that the reign of God, come among the assembly in its liturgy, is one of joyful abundance, indeed superabundance. If God's love knows no end, then joy too knows no end, and it is a genuine hallmark of the gatherings of the people of God.

5

Principle III

Good Liturgy Celebrates Community and Expresses Our Identities

Anyone who has ever been to dinner on a Royal Navy ship, even if that ship is a base on dry land, knows that the loyal toast is, uniquely, drunk while sitting down. This is usually explained as the result of the low ceilings in the cabins of the ships in Admiral Nelson's day, but if the height of the ceilings has changed, the ritual has not! It is now as much an expression of that group's identity as of loyalty. On another tack, is there a pastor who on arrival in a community has not been told that the way he has done something is "not how we do it *here*"? This duel over a ritual detail is usually only resolved when that minister accepts (or appears to accept) the status quo! But the real duel relates to the minister's willingness to identify with the community on its terms because some in the group see this as part of what is special about them.

For good or ill, Christian liturgy, just like the rituals of every human society ever studied by anthropologists, expresses the identity of the group. But if that is a fact, then why think of it in terms of being a principle. The reason we cannot think of liturgy expressing identity as just a fact is because identity, and celebrating identity, are very problematic, call for particular sensitivity, and must always involve reflection about why we have gathered for worship.

Several Extremes

For just about five hundred years the issue of the connection between liturgy and identity has been a fault line in the worship of western Christians. On one side has been the Catholic position that the liturgy should look and sound identical wherever and whenever it was celebrated. The myth was that a Catholic could go into a church building in Manhattan or Manchuria and "would feel at home." Liturgy was above culture, and particularity was indicative of a defect: a fissure in the unity of the church. The reality experienced was less spectacular than the ecclesiological claim. The liturgy was detached from whichever group celebrated it, in a language that was alien to the mother tongues of all.[1] Its claim to be isolated from culture obscured the fact that it was a very particular expression of the elite culture of Baroque Italy, and so it was one culture displacing in a colonial fashion every other culture. While its claim to uniformity was true at the textual level, the actual way that the liturgy was performed took on local colors. Ritual in a rural Spanish or Irish village was very different from that in a French or German city, but such differences were passed over as "noise" and zealous bishops tried

---

1. The extent to which Latin was a foreign language varied across Europe, but the fundamental fact was that the Catholic liturgy rejected the notion of the ordinary speech of the participants.

repeatedly to Romanize the liturgy and to install para-liturgical devotions after an Italian pattern without acknowledging that that was not some neutral universal culture but a specific expression of faith that was simply being given paradigm value.

By contrast, the churches of the Reformation stressed the local. It was this church, in this realm, with its own language, and foreign styles, rules, music, or personnel were just that: foreign. The *foreign* took on the same pejorative undertones that the *particular* took on for Catholics. Here was a local church that was imagined as being like the churches Paul founded around the Aegean, each self-governing and an expression before God of who the people gathered were. Rather than being tied to a uniformity, they saw themselves as being led by the Spirit, giving utterance to the depths of the spiritual life of those assembled. Moreover, the very variety of such ecclesial expressions—ranging from the highly structured Episcopalian liturgies to the spontaneity of charismatic worship and the near silence of Quaker meetings—was seen as an indicator that each was an expression of the genius of the community. Again, the reality was less than the theological claims. Each became fixed forms and showed that dislike of change that is characteristic of human rituals. Similarly, they became very much the expressions of particular groups and markers of the social, economic, and political vision of those communities and, when brought to new situations, linked back to the political and social situations in which they arose.

Eastern Christians have, traditionally, seen themselves as having a sense of the *oikoumene* made up of several more local churches—each with its own ritual, language, and patriarch—in communion. Perhaps here the need for liturgy to express the community is just not an issue because the liturgy is a little glimpse into heaven and barely touches the earth; I know several Orthodox theologians who would argue just this case. However, once again, having worship that is linked into a local community is more complex than having an explanatory ecclesiology. One can have a very high level of identification with a church and its tradition, because this is often part and parcel of religion being a cultural and ethnic glue, without the actual worship being an expression of the community of the baptized who are gathered. The whole community may be very defensive of what they are doing simply because ritual links to historical, cultural, and ethnic identity and so abhors any change that could be interpreted as a betrayal of a much loved inheritance. But does that mean that the whole group has a common vision of what they are doing? Moreover, is their assembly's worship linked to their vocation to be the people of God in the actual historical situation in which they find themselves?

Culture not only relates to what is inherited from the past such as language, ethnicity, and traditions but is itself dynamic. It is evolving and fluid and its boundaries are far fuzzier than conservative defenders of tradition are often prepared to admit. A liturgy that has become frozen in a moment may be staunchly defended—even by people with little involvement with the life of faith—but that should not be confused with expressing before God who we are, as disciples of Jesus, in this place today. It is from this authenticity of being "us" now that we offer praise, seek help, and strive to make sense of our lives in the light of the Gospel.

So where are we today? Most Christians today find themselves in a situation with regard to the culture around them that is very different from that of just a century ago. For most of our history, Christians, east and west, have been either the sole formal religious group or else have been in a binary situation of "us and them," the foreigners being seen as religious oppressors. In the first case, liturgy supplies cohesion to the whole society and its maintenance is a political matter; in the second, liturgy becomes a national marker of identity where change and adaptation is tantamount to treason. Today most churches still have many liturgical problems that are a legacy from that cultural situation. However, most Christians today live in multicultural situations: Christianity is just an option among others, and in many societies religion itself is seen as an option. This situation of pluralism is far more akin to the sort of world Paul of Tarsus knew than that known by our grandparents. But it means that whenever we talk about community, identity, and celebration, there is often an underlying tension between a vision of ritual that is an expression of ethnic continuity and one of ritual giving expression to a deliberate decision for the Gospel. When ritual is viewed in terms of ethnic continuity, it tends to be resistant to change and suspicious of imports, whether they are people or ideas. When liturgy is an expression of an option by those taking part, it tends to find cultural inheritance as little more than baggage. Negotiating these poles is a task as urgent as it is difficult.

We have to recall that the primary task of liturgy is to express where we as participants are, both as individuals and as bearers of the unique missionary vocation given to each person who follows Jesus. This missionary dimension means that the liturgy needs to be outgoing and willing to embrace new cultures and people. Again, this is a tension that was familiar to the first Christian communities, but it has only returned to the forefront of debate for many churches (apart from what were known as "the foreign missions") in recent decades.[2] The question of the link between liturgy and the

---

2. Thomas O'Loughlin, "Sharing Food and Breaking Boundaries: Reading of Acts 10–11:18 as a key to Luke's ecumenical agenda in Acts," *Transformation* 32 (2015): 27–37.

community's identity is now, once again, far more complex than any of the ecclesiological debates about local versus universal that have kept theologians writing and churchmen fighting for over a millennium.

Whose Community?

When we celebrate a liturgy in most WEIRD (*w*estern, *e*ducated, *i*ndustrial [and so urban], *r*ich, *d*emocratic) cultures today, we are rarely a single cultural unity in the way that a medieval village or a nineteenth-century German or Irish town was a cultural unit. The gathering may have many ethnic identities, possibly—and almost certainly in an urban situation—several mother tongues, and many different attitudes toward the place of ritual in life. A pastor can be confronted in quick succession with a middle-aged couple who would like a study-session focused on the gospels and social policy, an immigrant couple who want a medal blessed for their baby's stroller, someone who wants more incense and Latin chant, and someone else who wants to set up a novena to the Divine Mercy. These are not simply differing liturgical preferences: they manifest radically different, unformalized fundamental theologies, cultures, and visions of time, human agency, and the future. Indeed, apart from geographical proximity and self-identification with a particular religious tradition, there is very little that could be said about them as "a community." So, if liturgy is to be a genuine expression of oneness in Christ, what are we to do?

A simple first step is for those who lead liturgy to keep this issue in their minds as they set about their work. It can sometimes come as a shock to pastors how the official, book-based liturgy—ostensibly what everyone has come to celebrate—can be simply a formal screen devoid of depth in terms of the involvement of those making up the assembly. An extreme case of this was recounted by Hugh Brody when he wrote about a funeral in a First Nations' community in Canada. The actual community had a deep sense of their identity and with it a view of time, ritual, death and an understanding of what they were doing. The Catholic officials—the local priest and schoolteacher (both outsiders from a very different culture)—had theirs, which belonged to a world probably far closer to that of most who read this book. The two rituals just passed one another by! Here is Brody's description:

> When [the priest] had said some prayers, one of the schoolteachers began to read a long passage from the Bible. The shouts and footfalls of children now playing tag in the main part of the hall added to the noise. The man lying at the back did not stir. The service just carried on, the priest and teachers doing it their way, while the Indians did it theirs.[3]

There were two communities there in one location; there were indeed two liturgies going on there with just a few common elements such as concern with the corpse, and the rituals were abrading one another. Few liturgies are, thankfully, as broken up as this, but it is very silly to imagine that because all have come to one place at a specific time, that there is, *ipso facto*, any deep sense of being one people with a common origin in the Christ and his baptism, or a common vision of life or destiny. Ministers should probably

3. Hugh Brody, *Maps and Dreams: Indians and the British Columbia Frontier* (Vancouver, BC: Douglas and McIntyre, 1981): 79; the whole chapter, pp. 72–84, should be mandatory reading for anyone who wants to take on the role of presider!

always have had this awareness, though it is easy to see why it would not be at the front of the mind of someone who lives in a stable monocultural situation, but today it is a key to sensitive and successful liturgical leadership.

In seeking to address this situation of what we mean by community in the WEIRD world, one important "solution" is to develop liturgies that follow the ethnic and cultural contours of an area. This is *de facto* what happens not just when a particular ethnic group go to a liturgy in their own, nonmajority, language with a cleric from that community (my local parish has a "Polish Mass" once a month and a "Filipino Mass" when a priest from the Philippines is available), but when there are liturgies for young families, those who want certain styles of liturgy, or other groups with very defined identities (e.g., veterans) who want to give that identity an explicitly religious expression. The strength of this approach is that it starts with a human social reality and brings it into the sphere of the holy: grace building upon, rather than being in opposition to, nature. It recognizes an aspect of our humanity—such as how children experience group situations or how adults experience cultural style: be that a preference for folk music or polyphony—and allows this to be part of our liturgical encounter with one another, as disciples, and with God.

But while this is a widely practiced approach in Catholic worship today—and has a much longer history in the liturgies of other western churches—and its pastoral benefits are obvious, it is also worth reflecting on its limits. It can easily become a sanctification of our own views of society or even our views of our group's superiority to others around us. Yet, any liturgy where the values of the Gospel do not challenge our received attitudes is defective. While participating in the earthly liturgy, we must be continually open to how we, as groups, are in need of reform. The liturgy in first-century Corinth was one that took full account of the differing community identities (rich/poor, slave owner/slave, probably Jew/Gentile) but for Paul this was a denial of the Good News, for they were called to be one in Christ (1 Cor 10:17). There is also the risk that it can absolutize such notions as a "nation" as part of the divine plan. Neither the perception of the divine, nor the Gospel, nor the status of religion as a human reality is enhanced when our prayer reinforces divisions between groups in society or between countries. Christians are called to have an ambivalent attitude to all such loyalties; they are both in the world and bearing witness before the world to a vision of the Kingdom. Another problem is that such group liturgies can easily become excluding. This is not a problem when it is simply a matter of opting-in if it suits you (e.g., the Polish Mass when all the favorite Polish hymns can be sung), but liturgies with a high sectional definition can degenerate from the worship of God, creator of all, into celebrating our cultural icons. We can easily end up worshipping our culture through the medium of God!

While we should celebrate our cultural bonds and invoke the whole richness of human culture, we should also recall that our identity in liturgy is ultimately derived from our baptism—and baptism can embrace everyone. We are not just a people with an inherited religion, nor an old people with a new religion, but we are a new people: and we start on the task/challenge/vocation to become that new people each time we assemble.

Openness and Identity

Is there another approach? We tend to think of a gathering celebrating liturgy as an already existing community who then chose to do something: celebrate a particular liturgy. Perhaps our ideal should be to start at the other end and draw the actual gathering together such that they recognize themselves as a community in Christ because they are there engaging in worship. This is a challenge both as a piece of communication and as catechesis, but it accords with our deepest instincts as Christians that liturgy should not only express community but build the new community of disciples. This endeavor starts from the reality of what we are doing when we gather. Each person is a member of the people of God, as much as a member of the priestly people as anyone else, and the worship should be the common offering of all those present. This is a very different vision of the gathering from that of the liturgy being really that which the priest does, while the congregation are "in attendance" (the pre-Vatican II model), or that of liturgy being that of a special few, the people with specific tasks (the presider, the readers, the choir) or "the worship team," who "put on" a liturgy for the others' benefit (a model that fits our consumerist society). If we are the people of God, and each one of us made a daughter or son by adoption, then every liturgy must be *our* liturgy and so that of each and every one present.

This is the great goal of "full and active participation" called for by Vatican II. So the task is to let us discover, perhaps through a question-and-answer session, in this actual situation:

- how are we a community—why have such a variety of individuals come to one place;
- what is it that characterizes us as "us" here;
- what have each of us present to offer to the others today;
- how should we express *on this occasion* whatever identity we have found;

- how should that which is standard and inherited be adapted to the spontaneity by this moment;
- what should be the tone and flavor of our worship on this occasion?

Such an approach presents the presider, and those with the presider, with a set of challenges that go way beyond what most people think of as preparation for the liturgy, and actually putting it into effect may often be beyond what can be done in a large gathering on a Sunday morning. But it is not beyond what can be done in smaller groups and for specific occasions; and when it succeeds it can change "mere ritual" into an experience of *communitas* and grace.[4] Here, difficulties aside, lies one of the deepest challenges in renewal of the church. And, if we lose sight of that challenge, we will also miss out on how good liturgy can be transformative. The hope of all good liturgy is that when people are leaving the gathering they will have a sense—sometimes in words, sometimes without words—that "this has been our liturgy" and the "our" is linked to the actual community that has come into existence around the Lord's table.

At this point let's note that one big obstacle in the way of this vision of liturgy is size: the actual number of people present. Many Catholics are so used to very large gatherings—many hundreds gathered at one time—we forget that liturgy that allows for genuine participation requires much smaller gatherings. We have inherited a style that just did not consider this issue. The pre-1970 rite was the same whether

4. See Victor Turner, *The Ritual Process: Structure and Anti-Structure* (Hawthorne, NY: Aldine de Gruyter, 1995 [first published, 1969]), 131–65. Turner wrote about *communitas* many times but this chapter is a good introduction.

there was just one person there (the legal minimum) or hundreds of thousands (as at eucharistic congresses). Equally, we experience many situations of consumer performances (e.g., at a movie or a sports event) where one can easily scale up without affecting the individual experience (or, indeed, where the sheer volume of people adds to the experience). But the nature of liturgy—fundamentally shaped around a table—requires much smaller gatherings where we not only refer to one another as sisters and brothers, but actually have the opportunity of meeting those with us, if only for that one occasion. We need to fit the numbers of the ordained to the number of communities, not vice versa.[5]

Constant Tensions

Good liturgy must express and create community, but given that our society is not homogeneous and, indeed, those claiming one faith may be riven by distinctions based on wealth, ecclesiastical status, color, ethnicity, gender, and sexual orientation, we are confronted by a series of challenges that have to be held in tension. We must give expression to all the variety that actually exists while proclaiming the new, all-embracing identity in Jesus. We need to note the role of ethnicity and inheritance, while noting that such identities are not unchanging and can be damaging. We need to keep the tension of the *oikoumene* and the local, along with that of what is "in the book" with the needs of this group now and the tension between a sense of community defined historically by origins and that of a community defined by common hope and destination. We can express this tension

---

5. Thomas O'Loughlin, "How many priests do we need?," *New Blackfriars* 86 (2005): 642–57.

in two watchwords. First: think global; act local. Second: table is history; food is future. Every gathering at a table is an expression of history—it is common past experiences that have brought us there, but eating food is an expression of our needs for the future: energy to take us further along an as yet untrodden road.

6

Principle IV

Good Liturgy Facilitates Engagement

The need to have the correct set of clothes for the common event—in this case supporting your football team—is not a minor matter. One must have the right jersey along with the scarf (for waving rather than wearing) and know the right chants—for that is what supporters (note the word: it is more than is conveyed by "fans" and much more than conveyed by "onlookers") must do. Not to do so would mean that one was not really there nor engaged in supporting one's team. One does not go to a game simply to watch others play: one knows one is going to be engaged, to take part as a true supporter of a specific team.

The Way We Were

No topic in liturgy has generated more debate than the notion of what constitutes "engagement" or "participation." For centuries Catholics were simply required to *attend* or *hear* Mass on Sundays and holy days, but no one ever suggested that they should *take part* in the liturgy. Liturgy belonged to the priesthood (and perhaps monks and religious). Nonclergy might perform necessary tasks—serving or singing—but this engagement was peripheral to the actual work, and such engagement was to be considered as equivalent to a pianist having someone to turn the pages. Moreover, not only was the liturgy in a foreign language, employing an elaborate, arcane ritual, there seemed little need to do much to make it user friendly. Liturgy was done *by* the priest *for* the people. He acted on behalf of the people; it was the priest's work, or indeed Christ's work, but it was not the work of the people. Indeed, the liturgy would occur even if no one apart from the priest were there (although he needed a server "to answer" by rote). So the task for generations was not helping people to engage in the liturgy but to keep their minds within a religious frame with an activity parallel to the liturgy, such as reciting the rosary, saying other prayers, looking at the images, or listening to the music and, since such strategies were never very successful, to perform what people had to attend in the shortest time possible. This meant that "low" Mass—virtually always the normal experience—never lasted any more than 25–35 minutes (depending on the time of year) and never less than 12–20 minutes (also depending on the time of year)—and a layperson only had to be there from the time of the offertory until the priest drank the cup—at which point a bell rang to let people know they could now depart. Thus the minimum could be between 7 and 10 minutes (depending on the time of year and the priest's fluency in silently reading Latin).

This minimal view of participation as attendance—just being there—with its complete absence of deliberate mindful engagement was a bone of contention at the time of the

Reformation. But the Protestant insistence on conscious group engagement—most famously expressed in hearing Bible readings and prayers, coupled with singing hymns, in one's mother tongue—was seen as a two-pronged assault on (a) the objectivity of the sacraments and (b) the reality of the powers given uniquely to priests. The Council of Trent replied by insisting on even more uniformity, questioned (to the point of *de facto* outlawing) drinking from the cup,[1] and insisted on using Latin. So the characteristics of Catholic worship were that they needed "priests" (*sacerdotes*)—not just pastors or presbyters—who had "the power of order" and they took place in Latin. It would take centuries for Catholics to rediscover that the liturgy is the task/work/ celebration of all the baptized acting in Christ in praising the Father. Moreover, this awakening (beginning in tiny ways in France and Germany in the late nineteenth century) would only spread very slowly and hesitatingly until the time of the Second Vatican Council (1962–65).

Active Participation

Vatican II reminded Catholics that the liturgy is the public worship, the *leitourgia*, of the baptized and all are called to conscious, full, and "active participation."[2] And it was to facilitate this new vision of who we are as the church that the reformed liturgy appeared in 1969, and Latin, for the most part, disappeared. Contrary to persistent myth, the reform

---

1. Trent, Session XXI (July 16, 1562).
2. This term was used in *Sacrosanctum Concilium* 30, 41, and 50; and again in the curial documents that gave effect to the council's constitution: e.g., in *Musicam Sacram* (March 5, 1967) 15, again in *Eucharisticum Mysterium* (May 25, 1967), ch. 1, G-H.

was not democratization or "dumbing down" but a practical response to an awareness of just what we had forgotten that we should not have forgotten. If the liturgy is the collective service of "the one body" (1 Cor 10:17 and 12:12-13) of Christ, then one of the qualities of good liturgy is that it facilitates people's taking part in the activity, seeks ways to involve as many people as possible, and seeks out ways through which particular skills and viewpoints can be given expression. This is something that is grasped intuitively by many who have had to build a team, and it has been grasped in liturgies with particular groups (e.g., children), but this should be a conscious element in all liturgy planning. Since at least the time of the Council of Trent, one of the primary skills imparted in clerical training was that of effectively implementing the rubrics. In our era, a primary skill for anyone presiding at liturgy must be facilitating and encouraging the active participation of each person in the community present at an act of worship. It is a skill whose importance was implicitly recognized in Vatican II, but that has not yet become a recognized necessary skill in the self-perception of most clergy.

But—many argue—*active* does not mean that everyone has to have a job, to be doing something: this, they say, is to confuse *active* with *activism*; and that, whatever it means, is not good! While indeed one can participate by prayerful listening and silent rapt attention, we are also the people of the incarnation, of bodies as much as minds or spirits! And, as Aristotle sagely remarked, we engage most with that which engages us through the senses. The more we are engaged through the senses, the more we are engaged in what is happening around us.[3] The football match—which is very much

3. *Metaphysics* 1,1,1–6 (980a–981a); and cf. *Nicomachean Ethics* 3,10 (1117b–1118b).

a collective public work, a *leitourgia*—is a good analogy. Supporters are wholly engaged: watching (sight), singing and cheering (hearing/speech), jumping up and down and clapping (movement/touch), wearing emblems and commenting to fellow supporters (sight/speech), aware that they belong to a group (movement/touch/group contact), and it is the whole ensemble that makes a match worth going to. Likewise, if the senses are not engaged in worship, then most people will tend not to be engaged or engaged only in a very detached way. Some will not find this necessary or might even find it distracting; but most people are attracted more to sense-engaged worship (be that the vibrancy of evangelical singing or the senses-engaged activities of popular cults), than to the restrained reflection one can find in the liturgy of many monastic communities. Hence a practical test of good liturgy is that it finds ways to draw as many of the gathering as possible into having a sense of taking part, having something to contribute to the activity, and something that stirs hands and feet, as well as mind and spirit.

It is all too easy to dismiss cynically a liturgy that involves, in some practical way, everyone present as mere hectic doings replacing interiority. But, first of all, it is a great achievement to so motivate people to engage. Second, grace builds on human nature rather than working against the grain of our humanity. And, most importantly, we can take another perspective: viewing each of those practical doings as a particular manifestation of the diverse gifts of the Holy Spirit in our worship.

The Spirit Empowers

We can go even further and say that a good liturgy makes everyone feel—*feeling* being a whole-person experience—

that this is our liturgy and this is our community, not just that of the church or the special group or the priest. Any liturgy, or activity in a liturgy, that creates a sense of community is an empowering event. As such, it continues and sends forth the saving work of the Anointed One. And when—as we know from other spheres of life[4]—everyone does something, then the assembly powerfully becomes *our* public work, *our* project, *our* liturgy. The task of those who lead liturgy is not simply to make people feel part of what is going on (such inclusivity is just a starting point), nor to help keep them focused (liturgy is celebration of love, not a religious work-out) but that of empowering all present. We have to move from interest in attendance to actualizing participation, to facilitating empowerment.

4. It has been noted that if many people have been involved in creating—using the wiki principle—a community map, then the common task is not just creative of a new sense of community but has an empowering effect on all present; see Jiri Panek, "From Mental Maps to GeoParticipation," *Cartographic Journal* 53 (2016): 301.

7

Principle V

Good Liturgy Is Inclusive

My friend's invitation, "Let's have lunch in my club," seemed little more than a convenient option. On arrival I had to be signed in by a member (my host), and while this was taking place I spotted the notice about attire. This did not bother me as I was in work mode and so wearing a tie and jacket. The custom was to have pre-lunch drinks in the foyer: very pleasant. But whenever my host turned away, one or other club member, seeing me standing alone, would politely, but with a definite interrogative tone, ask, "Are you alright?" The reply that I was with my friend removed their anxiety and they passed on. The queries were not so much after my welfare as checks on a frontier. They were challenging me lest I did not realize that I was not a member of *their* club; they were insiders and I was not. For décor, cuisine, and, indeed, the wit of the conversation, one would travel far to find such a fine club, but one would never accuse them of being inclusive. I did not feel welcome and that feeling of being alien affected my demeanor and slightly antagonized me toward all that "they" stood for.

Compared with other forms of discrimination based on color, ethnicity, gender, or sexual orientation—where blood is shed and lives are ruined through notions of superiority/inferiority, or the effects of notions of caste with its grades of purity/impurity—the feeling of being a trespasser in a club that traded on its exclusivity is just a trifle—comic in many respects—but it is also a reminder that we can pay lip-service to notions of human equality, or the explicitly Christian view that we are all children of God, but fail to notice our day-to-day rejections of others. Indeed, even the liturgy—which should be Christians on their best behavior—can take on human biases, exclusivities, and discriminations and make them normative. Why is the presence of such exclusivities important? Because the liturgy repeatedly performs a vision of society, and by its repetition it forms and informs our vision of life; its repetition inscribes a vision of society in the core of our identity.[1] This is also why early Christians were concerned that the Eucharist should not become exclusive: God shows no partiality! (Rom 2:11 and Acts 10:34).[2]

If there is latent discrimination in a ritual—and rituals have been called "staged cultural expressions"[3]—then its performance tells all involved that this behavior, this exclusivity/discrimination is not only OK, but has divine sanction. We might think that such blindness belongs only in extreme situations (as during the time of Apartheid in South Africa) or in faraway countries (for example, among Christians in

1. Paul Connerton, *How Societies Remember* (Cambridge: Cambridge University Press, 1989), 72–104.

2. Thomas O'Loughlin, "Sharing Food and Breaking Boundaries: Reading of Acts 10–11:18 as a key to Luke's ecumenical agenda in Acts," *Transformation* 32 (2015): 27–37.

3. M. E. Combs-Schilling, *Sacred Performances: Islam, Sexuality and Sacrifice* (New York: Columbia University Press, 1989), 30.

India today there can be two queues at the time of receiving communion: one for the "purer" castes and another for the untouchables[4]). However, it can slip into any gathering almost unnoticed so that anyone who is not part of the in-group cannot but pick up the vibes: *you* are not one of *us*.

Rituals of Separation

Why is the liturgy so prone to becoming an exercise in excluding people? One of the basic moves of all human ritual is that of dividing: the clean from the unclean, the sacred from the profane, the holy from the unholy, "them" from "us." These notions have all too often been imported into Christian worship, both consciously (imagining the liturgy in terms of the temple in Jerusalem as exemplified in the language Christians have used) and unconsciously (as in notions of impurity and purification). But here lies one of the great discontinuities between the Gospel and human religious consciousness: the Christ has overcome the divisions (Gal 3:28), the curtain of the temple has been torn asunder (Mark 15:38), and all the baptized form a priestly people (1 Pet 2:9). Our liturgy, as Paul reminded the Corinthians, proclaims that we are one in Christ (1 Cor 10). So if divisiveness is part of our liturgical assemblies, we may be responding to our unconscious, but not to the Gospel.

Baptism Establishes a New Set of Relationships

No one from among the baptized should go away from a liturgy feeling that she or he was excluded, cut off, or estranged. When that happens, the fundamental dynamic of the liturgy as a

---

4. Antony Susai Raj, "Dalits at the Eucharistic Table," *Japan Mission Journal* 68, no. 1 (2014): 12.

celebration of reconciliation has been fatally compromised. Yet all too often the most felt perception of individuals at a liturgy is that of exclusion: exclusion due to theological background, sexual orientation, marital status, or a sense that a liturgy is the property of a particular group. If that is the perception, then the liturgy has failed for that individual, and if that perception has a basis in the behavior of the larger group then their liturgy has become a counter-sign to the Gospel of love.

While many might assert that their communities are welcoming, and indeed reconciling, it should not be forgotten how easily attitudes of them/us, toward those who are "active participants" vs. those who merely "attend" can appear within our worship. Liturgy must be consciously nondivisive and must equally consciously promote a sense of oneness in Christ. So what signal does the spatial location of clergy/ministers in relation to laity/ministered-to send to both groups? In monastic churches, is there a choir of monastics with the visitors located elsewhere? This may correspond to the reality that for the monastics, this is home, while everyone else is a visitor to the monastery, but in the liturgical space all are equally sisters and brothers in the family of baptism—and so should, in the context of liturgy, not be segregated. We are claiming, theologically, a new set of relationships in liturgy; the least we can do is to express it in the seating plan!

But Is It That Important?

Whenever a deliberate attempt is made to see if a group's liturgy is inclusive, someone will object that this is merely pandering to minority hang-ups; so what if someone doesn't feel welcomed, it's not about feelings! Someone else will say that it is just marketing, a ploy to attract people with surface perceptions, and that faith is deeper than this. And a third objector will point out that the church has a moral code and that somehow inclusivity is undermining that standard; inclusivity is condoning wickedness and betraying the past.

These are objections that are made seriously, but they are less conclusive on reflection than rhetorically. Let's begin with the objection that inclusivity is about feelings. Human beings gather most of the stimuli on which they make their decisions through their feelings. We generate a picture of those around us that allows us to relate to that world far more accurately than any detached rational analysis. If I feel I do not belong, chances are that there are many around me who feel the same way about me! But the new community we are seeking to create in Christian liturgy is one in which no child of God should feel this. We are seeking to emulate in flesh and blood, here and now, the welcome God extends to every creature. Just as people become alienated—which literally means being made to perceive oneself as a "foreigner"—from the divine through alienation from religion, so the welcome found in religion conveys something of the divine. This mission entrusted to the church calls us, on the one hand, to be self-conscious that we are not causing people to feel alienated, and, on the other hand, to deliberately hold out the hand of welcome, that through our welcome a sister or brother might experience the hand of God.

Centuries ago Thomas Aquinas was wont to invoke two key ideas about human knowing, perception, and growth: firstly, that whatever I perceive comes into my consciousness with modifications due to the kind of person I am, and, secondly, that what I think about comes to me through my senses.[5] These could also serve as rules of thumb by those

5. Both of these became dicta within the tradition: the first was expressed as *quidquid recipitur secundum modum recipientis recipitur* and the second as *nihil in intellectu nisi fuerit in sensu.*

who lead liturgies. If I am to be welcomed, and part of the community that celebrates, remembers, and offers a collective act of thanksgiving, then I must feel welcomed if I am to commit myself to the communal action and actively and consciously participate. Feelings and perceptions are not secondary. I must perceive myself being made one with others if I am to wholeheartedly act with them. Put negatively, if I perceive that I am not included in the common action, then I cannot actively participate—or else I would be deluding myself to say, "I belong," when all the evidence reaching me says the opposite. We, the group who feel we do belong, must be aware that the love of God reaches to every creature that God's love holds in existence. If God loves that creature, then we must welcome that creature. God does not retain us as his bouncers.

The notion that inclusivity is a call to use exclusions as a way of proclaiming a moral law is an objection of a different kind because it is far more closely related to a deep strand of human ritual that sees collective worship as an expression of exclusive belonging. Here a group, a tribe or nation, or some gathering imagine themselves as the elect—the ones God has chosen—in distinction to those God has rejected. Such partiality has bedeviled Christian theology—some group or other claiming to be God's own or to have an exclusive claim on truth—since the very earliest churches.[6] Moreover, there is a long history in the churches of seeking to use exclusion from the liturgy as a form of punishment. Was this practice of excommunication simply mistaken? The answer to that is too complex for a book on liturgy. It suffices to note here that that practice was based on two assumptions. First,

---

6. See Acts 6:1—and the early Christian slogan: "God shows no partiality" (Acts 10:34; Rom 2:11; Gal 2:6; Eph 6:9; Col 3:25; and Jas 3:17).

within those societies public worship was simply a given; when God's existence is not questioned, then one can use exclusion as a threat that might "bring someone to their senses." (Whether or not one should use threats, or whether threats ever bring about the conversion of heart that is the subject of the Gospel's call, are separate questions.) The second assumption underlying exclusion as a penalty is that all concerned view taking part in the liturgy as a necessary duty. When that view prevails, then exclusion can be seen as unwillingness to condone unacceptable behavior.

However, once we are in a society where commitment to God is viewed as an option, the work of the faithful has to take on a missionary dimension. The way the assembled community of faith behaves has to model to the larger society the universality of God's loving care and interest. Our welcome must proclaim that God is love, and that God wills all to be saved and none to be excluded. Similarly, if we conceive of liturgy as a joyful response to God's loving invitation, rather than the fulfillment of an imposed duty, then we have to re-formulate how we think of any act of exclusion. Exclusion or discrimination is now tantamount to saying that God's invitation is not to all. Conversely, we must see any willingness to join with us as a stirring, prompted by the Holy Spirit, in that person's heart to respond to the divine. Our inclusivity and welcome should recall that the Christ "welcomes sinners and eats with them" (Luke 15:2). In our situation, if someone shows a desire to be with us, we must honor that willingness to join us as a stirring of the Spirit—and respond with welcome.

The Hospitality of God

This quality of liturgy means that a primary concern of any community, large or small, should be to manifest itself as welcoming and open. Just as the Good News embraces all humanity, so the communities' response to the Gospel must convey a sense of welcome to all, but especially to the marginalized. Sectarian behavior, such as "we are the elect," can all too easily become a binding element in a community, but it is its opposite that should be the marker of a healthy liturgy. Liturgical inclusivity is an expression of the hospitality of God.

8

Principle VI

Good Liturgy Is Based in the Creation

The act of turning on lights by flicking a switch is so simple for us as to be almost mindless. We just get the light level right, and lighting is everywhere. But the action of lighting lamps or candles from a living flame—itself perhaps the result of striking a spark—was a very definite moment in the evening: day was done, time was moving on, darkness was approaching. In a monastery that moment might have been greeted by a very formal ritual: the *lucernarium*, but in a peasant's home it was more likely greeted by the prayer: "May God give us the light of heaven." This prayer's simplicity hides its profundity. For those looking at the lighted lamp, the prayer implicitly states that all good things, such as light, come from God, and we should acknowledge that origin thankfully. For those looking through the light, it affirms the reality of our world; the lighted lamp is brightening our room, the very room where we are living and eating and talking; and, reflectively, it grasps that this little light is a sacrament to another reality, greater-than-this-existence that beckons us.

It might seem a tautology for a monotheist to make this point. Where else could liturgy be based except in the creation? After all, is not everything around us a gift of God?

> All things came to be through him,
>   and without him nothing came to be.
> What came to be through him was life,
>   and this life was the light of the human race;
> the light shines in the darkness,
>   and the darkness has not overcome it. (John 1:3-5)

However, in our celebrations we easily (and often) slip into thinking in a series of binaries: the material world as distinct from the spiritual realm, the actual things of liturgy as distinct from the ideas they want to affirm, the mere signs as distinct from the realities they point to, and that very subtle schism of ritual versus reality. When such binary thinking catches hold, the liturgy can easily turn into a kind of game in which nothing is really what it is and everything is a kind of code for something else. When this happens, "understanding the liturgy" is transformed into a game with a group of initiates "decoding" symbols to re-encode them as strings of words and ideas. In the long run, the liturgy seems like a puzzle for children in which, once the underlying ideas have been absorbed, the actual engagement in the liturgy can be left as optional or as demanding only the bare minimum.

Last Holy Thursday I heard a perfect example of this. Real reality was the love of the Father and the Son, the heavenly banquet was a code to explain this, the Last Supper was a code to explain the heavenly banquet, the Mass was a code for the Last Supper—that was the sermon; then came the time to actually share in the banquet. The priest took a ciborium from the tabernacle (never mind this was the one day the rubrics say to have it empty before you begin) and each had a wafer unlike any real bread we ever tasted, and only the priest drank from the cup. Many got lost during the sermon, and I doubt that anyone could feel any link between what we ate and our experience of a feast or banquet. The signs—the several complex layers of them—were divorced from our creaturely experience. This liturgy was not rooted in the creation.

Starting from **Within** *the Creation*

One of the most basic facts of human beings is not that they eat together but that they share meals. Meal sharing is something we do—and doing it we bind ourselves to one another, we mark significant events in our lives, and we enjoy ourselves. We do not do this *in order to* do something else (such as bond with those we love), but simply because we do it and like doing it. Bonding with those around us is a consequence. People can use meals deliberately for this or that purpose, but before one can use a meal one has to be pretty sure that meals are part of our human way of being! Just so, it is the basic reality of being thankful for our food and our company that leads us to acknowledge God at our meals. To be "us" is to be meal sharing, and to be thankful. "Blessed is the Lord, the God of all creation, through his goodness we have this food . . . " This is the basic form of domestic communal prayer for Jews and Christians. If we are to be a people of thankfulness—a eucharistic people—then being aware of the creation, affirming the creation and its goodness, and valuing it as a divine gift, are at the heart of our liturgy. So when we do food we are engaging in the creation; when we so engage, we, as believers, should be thankful—and thankfulness values the creation.[1]

---

1. See Thomas O'Loughlin, *The Eucharist: Origins and Contemporary Understandings* (London: Bloomsbury T&T Clark, 2015), 61–94.

Often we claim to be taking part in a banquet, but use such token amounts of food that it is hard to imagine we are serious. We claim to reside in the world made through the Logos but use a language that shuns the earthy and familiar as somehow unworthy of the sacred. We talk about symbols but do not engage as creatures with these parts of the creation. By contrast, if all aspects of our humanity have been redeemed, then our human situation—such as the human desire to share meals—should form the basis of our formal liturgy. Put another way, if we really believe that Jesus is God coming among us, then we can be elbow to elbow with the divine when we eat. Liturgy must give us the vision that allows us to see this, not just at the table in the church, but to be open to it at every table.

Engagement with Creation

Being thankful *for* creation is at the heart of theism. Living with the awareness that God had entered *into* creation is at the heart of Christianity. And, given our modern culture's power, being responsible *with* creation is part of contemporary discipleship.

This need to engage responsibly, knowing that we can destroy our world and cause suffering through exploitation, is part of discipleship today in a way unimaginable even a few decades ago. It is, for instance, no longer valid to appeal to the text in Genesis about "subduing the earth" because it is one thing to subdue a wild countryside with a hoe, quite another to destroy an ecosystem. Gradually we have been replacing the language of dominating and subduing with that of stewarding and taking responsibility. If this is a real development in our Christian understanding of the world, then it has to have a liturgical dimension for it is in the liturgy that we perform our vision of the creation.

What this means in practice will vary with our situations, but the basic challenge of this being a principle of good liturgy applies everywhere. Here are a couple of examples. We still use many texts in the liturgy that employ the preindustrial attitude of dominating and controlling the creation. These are simply inappropriate and we should stop using them (in the same way that we had to stop using texts that saw Jews as corporately guilty of the death of Jesus). Another example: we have many rituals that hover on the edge of the liturgy, such as harvest festivals or blessing of specific foods on certain days. Can we draw these more into the mainstream of our liturgical life, seeing them as expressions of a relationship to one another and the environment that is not just quaint and homespun, but celebrations that awaken us to a bigger picture? Likewise, when we pray for forgiveness for our failings or petition the Father for our needs, do we take responsibility for the decisions that damage the creation and remember those whose lives are being blighted by climate change? We are part of the creation, we acknowledge God as Creator, therefore we cannot duck ecology when we pray!

Liturgy should be ecologically sensitive, respect human justice, and perform for us as vision of ourselves as a people who can think beyond the immediate. Alas, the best way to observe the importance of this quality is by its absence. If a liturgy is not rooted in who we are as human beings, and part of that for all humanity today is the ecological crisis that confronts our planet, then its status as *our* worship in *our* historical situation is questionable.

9

Principle VII

Good Liturgy Prioritizes the Marginalized

The scene in the cathedral was splendid: every detail announced it was a great solemnity. The pews were packed with ordinary people; each had obtained a seat by ticket. Outside, guards kept others back at barriers. The central areas were reserved and filled from the back in strict precedence. At the front was the head of state's representative flanked by his aide-de-camp and a monsignor as a chaplain. The procession of clergy—itself a model of differing ranks—arrived, the cardinal bowed to the chief civil dignitary, and Mass began. It was splendid theatre and a performance of an ideal of an ordered and obedient society. All acted their parts with dedication and for many it was a very moving occasion; we humans easily confuse the solemn with the sacred. It was a celebration using Christian images and the rituals of Christian faith, but it left me with a niggling worry: Did it perform the Christ's vision of the people of God where the first is to be last, where God loves all equally as sisters and brothers?

It is all too easy for ritual to screen itself off from the lived reality of our own messy lives and of suffering humanity. When this happens it is no longer the public work of those who are committed to conveying liberation and redemption; it has become the refuge from reality that was rightly condemned by Marx when he pointed out that

> the social principles of Christianity justified the slavery of Antiquity, glorified the serfdom of the Middle Ages and equally know, when necessary, how to defend the oppression of the proletariat, although they make pitiful face over it.[1]

That "pitiful face" takes, very often, the form of words used in liturgy without any further engagement. But liturgy must touch on the marginalized in a practical way within its own praxis.

The Collection

The paradigm example of this concern for the poor is the fact that at the early eucharistic banquets there was a collection among the gathering for the care of the poor.[2] While the collection as a practice has remained, its focus has been subverted from care of the needy to support of the clergy and the administration, but a genuine expression of care for the poor should be part of every celebration. Moreover, this care of the poor was just as difficult for them as it is for

1. Karl Marx, "The Communism of the Paper *Rheinischer Beobachter*," in *On Religion*, by Karl Marx and Friedrich Engels (Moscow: Foreign Languages Publications House, 1957), 74.
2. See Justin, *Apologia prima* 67,6–7 (written probably in the period 145–155).

us: Paul, when he wrote to the Corinthians in the early fifties of the first century, was already worried about Christian gatherings taking on the social hierarchy of the surrounding society in which the rich ate their splendid food and the rest ate whatever was available.

Christian liturgy simply does not accept the notion that there are those who have and those who have not. The liturgy performs a vision of a society in which all are equally loved by God and so should benefit equally from God's goodness. Then, since it believes that we engage with faith in the actual world of everyday existence, it is not enough that we perform this new vision just inside the liturgy, but we must work toward it while at liturgy using practical means, and putting one's hand in a pocket for a collection of the poor in the very heart of a liturgy connects liturgy and the rest of life!

Put another way, insofar as all Christian liturgy needs to proclaim the absolute generosity of God, this must take material expression in human generosity. If I have even an inkling that God loves me, then it is only by loving generously—and in a money society that means acting with money—that I will come to understand this more deeply. And the reverse also holds true: any impression of that appreciation is false if it does not express itself by sharing actual resources. "If anyone says, 'I love God,' but hates his brother, he is a liar; for whoever does not love a brother whom he has seen cannot love God whom he has not seen" (1 John 4:20).

Practical Action; Generous Attitudes

Moreover, that generosity cannot be limited to providing resources for the poor—that is but a minimal and constant requirement—but must show the community actively relating to all who find themselves marginalized on the basis of race, color, gender, sexual orientation, disability, civic status, or whatever. Just as embracing all such marginalized people must be part of discipleship (Matt 25:31-40), so it must be a felt part of liturgy that claims to proclaim the redemption.

When a liturgy does not value the marginalized, it runs the danger of failing to recognize that social change is at the heart of Christianity in that it is a religion of salvation and that Jesus' message is one that sets existing social relationships on their head. He is among us as one who serves (Luke 22:27), so too we are among humanity proclaiming a new vision of service. Indeed, there is a strong case to be made that this is one aspect of discipleship to which Jesus gave ritual shape in footwashing, and it is worth noting how this has been an aspect of Christian ritual, albeit a peripheral one.[3]

Liturgy and Ethics, Chalk and Cheese!

I have met many experts in Christian ethics over the years who dismiss care over liturgy as almost a children's game. Likewise, I have met many devoted to liturgy and spirituality who have viewed social and moral questions as merely practical compared with their more lofty concerns. Indeed, this division has a long history among Christians, going back to Cassian's prioritizing *theoria* (concerning the spiritual) over *praxis* (concerning the material world). However, when we have an ethics without liturgy, the Good News can eas-

---

3. See Sandra M. Schneiders, "The Foot Washing (John 13:1–20): An Experiment in Hermeneutics," *Catholic Biblical Quarterly* 43 (1981): 76–92; and Thomas O'Loughlin, *Washing Feet: Imitating the Example of Jesus in the Liturgy Today* (Collegeville, MN: Liturgical Press, 2015).

ily become no more than a wrapper for a social philosophy.
Likewise, when the Good News has a liturgy that is not
simultaneously engaged with the situation of human beings
around us, then our liturgy ceases to be located in reality,
God's creation, becoming just a variant on an esoteric cult.
What we need is a liturgico-social vision.

The liturgy performs the society God wills for people
and it is that which we, as disciples of Jesus, proclaim as the
Good News. Commenting on Paul's criticism of the liturgy
in mid-first-century Corinth, one scholar summed up this
liturgico-social vision rather elegantly:

> The ritual of the Lord's Supper calls the participants to
> behavior based on values such as equality, rather than
> hierarchy; mutual servitude, rather than competition;
> and humility, rather than the upward mobility enshrined
> in the power structures of the Greco-Roman world.[4]

---

4. Rachel McRae, "Eating with Honor: The Corinthian Lord's
Supper in the Light of Voluntary Association Meal Practices," *Journal
of Biblical Literature* 130 (2011): 180.

10

Principle VIII

Good Liturgy Avoids Clutter

The little boy watched the ceremony of two servers washing the priest's hands after the presentation of the gifts and asked the catechist beside him in a too-loud voice, "Why didn't he wash his hands before he started?" "Because Pontius Pilate," she replied, "washed his hands before Jesus died on the cross and Jesus is going to die now for you and me!" "Jesus is going to die now—can we not stop him?" The catechist, clearly having given enough information, simply rubbed her head and, noticing that I was listening, gave me an embarrassed smile.

There are two ritual phenomena that are so obvious that we tend to miss them. First, liturgy tends to accumulate stuff far more easily than it gets rid of bits and pieces; and secondly, we build up our big pictures from the details of experience and, therefore, often come up with very odd explanations of what we are doing when we gather and celebrate.

Liturgical Practice Is "Sticky"

Every ritual tends to repeat what happened the last time and then adds something new, special, or specific. So a prayer is added for a special occasion, and then it gets stuck there and becomes a standard element. We use the same hymn on many occasions, and then find it hard to drop it, even when it is inappropriate to the event being celebrated. Or, we put an extra table out for a specific purpose and it just stays there, then gets used for something else, and then is assumed to be needed all the time! This is the "stickiness" of ritual that makes it steadily expand in complexity and details and involve ever more odds and ends that do not really fit with what we claim as our rationale for what we do.

This struck me forcibly on last Easter Sunday when looking up from the back of the church, it seemed that the whole sanctuary area was covered with flowers, expensive and large flowers: nothing less than lilies with their long stems and each vase filled out with other flowers. There was a big flower arrangement on the floor in front of the eucharistic table, which looked like a ledge behind the flowers. There was another big arrangement on each side: one in front of the ambo (now invisible) and another just in front of the chair, so the presider was invisible when he sat down. Two more were further back: out of one peered a cross and out of the other the paschal candle. That it was there and alight on Easter Sunday morning was not obvious because there were umpteen other candles burning (most of them there since before the 1970 restructuring). A spotlight played on the shining brass tabernacle door whose central position made it the visual focus of all that was happening, while a PowerPoint was on a screen to one side with the words of hymns interspersed with a cycle of generic Easter imagery. The whole seemed a bright floral stage from which emerged words, much as on every other Sunday, while the hymns were all well-known Mass hymns. The only noticeably different activity was the presider coming down the center aisle sprinkling water at one point. This seemed strange to most of the gathering because those who were "hit" with the water looked uncomfortable and sought to wipe it quickly from their faces.

Liturgy Is Open to Interpretations

The second phenomenon always at work when we take part in liturgy is our desire to draw all the bits of our experience into a story and to get that story to make some sort of sense within our bigger story. But the bits can sometimes add up to a story that does not sit very well with the Gospel! A bizarre example of this is what happened to the lavabo ritual, which was very visible in a liturgy that was almost silent. Originally, it was the presider's practical need to wash his hands, having handled all the foodstuffs that were presented before moving on to the eucharistic prayer. Later the foods (except for bread and wine) disappeared, but the washing remained. Then the presentation of even the bread and wine disappeared but still his hands were washed, but why bother? Had he not been told to wash his hands before vesting (at which point there was even a special prayer)? Moreover, since it no longer served a practical purpose, the act of having his hands washed for him became more elaborate, and to help make sense of this little sub-ritual, a set of prayers were added to the practice. But what were those who simply saw it to make of it? There were many explanations over the centuries, but this was a very popular one: just as Pilate washed his hands before the crucifixion (Matt 27:24), so does the priest, because he is about to have Jesus undergo his sacrifice once more.[1] It is still around: I heard that catechist just a few years ago. By its nature, ritual is open to endless interpretations. In this, liturgy is more akin to poetry than to prose. But when such an interpretation is arrived at, then we have gone beyond legitimate interpretation and into a dangerous fantasyland. Today, the lavabo ritual is really just clutter that we were too hesitant to drop in 1970.

Liturgy, Communication, and Proclamation

Every liturgy communicates—like it or not, for better or worse—and we need to examine, again and again, what message we are sending out. Moreover, we have to seek a harmony between the messages that can be taken away and the message, the Gospel of Jesus, that we are commissioned to preach. Just as Christians have to be aware of how they can be sending out wrong messages in formal teaching, so in what we do in the liturgy we have to make a conscious effort to avoid sending incorrect or jumbled messages. Likewise, we should be careful that we do not so overload our ritual communication that it ends up suggesting that everything is the same as everything else. I suspect that most of the wrong messages taken from the liturgy are the result of clutter, noise, and the distractions of missing the big picture because of so many bits that are just there because they happen to be there!

---

1. This allegorical explanation was quite mainstream; it can be found in influential thirteenth-century theologian William Durand (*Rationale* 4,28), which was mined for such explanations until well into the twentieth century; see Timothy M. Thibodeau, *William Durand: Rationale IV—On the Mass and Each Action Pertaining to it* (Turnhout: Brepols, 2013), 240.

An essential part of all ritual is communication.[2] And this communication should be capable of saying something about the Christian vision to every participant. Moreover, in an already noisy world, ritual should help us to focus. But consider the Easter morning scene I have just recalled: What is central, what is peripheral, and what is just clutter? Now pity the people who "get to church" only at Christmas. Just picture what their eyes take in. Directly in front of the eucharistic table is located the crib scene, near it is still to be found the paschal candle, and near it is a small baptismal font. Then there is the ambo, another lectern, several seats, and just behind them a Christmas tree, and the whole building is arranged in the oblong shape of an old-fashioned theatre rather than for a community celebration around the table of the Lord. What is just there, what is there for a special reason, what is the central activity for which people have gathered? Only an expert could answer these simple questions; but every visitor will come up with an answer! Has our way of doing helped such people to a better grasp of the Good News?

A first step to better proclamation within the liturgy is to see avoiding clutter as part of a good liturgy. On Easter Sunday make sure that the paschal candle—the light of the risen Lord—is big enough to stand out and cannot be confused with any number of other candles that happen to be there. Then let it be a reflective focus of our actions—perhaps by inviting each person to come up and light one's own candle from it in the manner of the Vigil before the Easter profession of faith, rather than just having it there as one

2. See Eric W. Rothenbuhler, *Ritual Communication: From Everyday Conversation to Mediated Ceremony* (Thousand Oaks, CA: Sage, 1998).

more bit of kit mandated by the rubrics. There may still be as many interpretations of it as there are participants—that is part of the mystery of liturgy—but at least it is not just a puzzle! By contrast, a liturgy full of distractions, unnecessary complications, or anachronistic curiosities diverts our focus from the divine mystery and our pilgrim path into a maze of curiosities.

11

Principle IX

Good Liturgy Follows the Pattern of the Incarnation

There is a tension at the heart of Christian liturgy that can be seen in the complete informality of some Christians' worship—where they consciously reject anything that smacks of ritual—and that of other equally sincere Christians that have a panoply of elaborate ritual, complex rules, and a great gulf between the ways of everyday life and the ways of worship. Down the centuries these two groups have often fought with each other (as, for example, in the aftermath of the Reformation) and tried to decide which was right, who was wrong, with both sides trying to prove their positions by appeals to the Bible or antiquity.[1] Neither side could ever win because there is a deeper tension we have to keep in mind.

1. Thomas O'Loughlin, "Divisions in Christianity: The Contribution of 'Appeals to Antiquity,'" in *Faithful Reading: New Essays in*

The tension is this. On the one hand, human beings develop rituals almost without noticing it, and these become built into our memories. As they are repeated they grow ever more complex, full of contradictions, elaborate, and further in appearance from the situations in everyday life that gave rise to them.[2] Moreover, the default setting of human religious consciousness is to define the religious or the holy by contrast with the creation, by its distance from the everyday, by its otherness. So often people speak of the divine realm as the wholly other.[3] Likewise, studies show that most human societies down through the centuries have imagined their encounters with the divine as occurring in a location other than where we actually live, and even in a special time that is not continuous with actual history.[4] In radical contrast to these recurrent human patterns of ritual, we have the Christian confession of faith: Jesus was a human being, an individual with a history, who was born in a specific place, and "suffered under Pontius Pilate." For Christians, God has entered history, has walked among us, spoken to us in our houses, in the fields nearby, along the road, at the well, and he has sat at our tables and there given us a way of offering a thanksgiving sacrifice to the Father in heaven. So we have the distance of the divine as a basic theme of human ritual

---

Theology and Philosophy in Honour of Fergus Kerr OP, ed. S. Oliver, K. Kilby, and T. O'Loughlin (London: T&T Clark, 2012), 221–41.

2. Paul Connerton, *How Societies Remember* (Cambridge: Cambridge University Press, 1989), 72–104; and Eric W. Rothenbuhler, *Ritual Communication: From Everyday Conversation to Mediated Ceremony* (Thousand Oaks, CA: Sage, 1998).

3. See Rudolf Otto, *The Idea of the Holy* (Oxford: Oxford University Press, 1923), for the classic exposition of this view.

4. This was a recurrent theme in the work of Mircea Eliade, e.g., *Myths, Dreams and Mysteries* (London: Harvill Press, 1960).

and the closeness of the divine as a basic element of Christian discipleship.

Liturgy has to acknowledge the human tendency to think of God as otherness but also remember the basic proclamation: "And the Word became flesh and set up his tent among us, and we have seen his glory" (John 1:14). We usually translate this as "he dwelled among us" or "he lived among us" but both of those translations miss the liturgical point. God's potent presence in Israel was the special tent (the tabernacle/tent of Exod 26) that was the place apart into which only a special few, the priests, might enter. Now the tabernacle/tent of encounter was a human being and that individual, Jesus, moved among us and brought all who joined him into the presence of God. When Jesus sat at the ordinary table in Zacchaeus's house (Luke 19:1-10), that table became as the altar in the temple, and so every table at which disciples eat was made a place where God could be encountered. "Today salvation has come to this house, because [Zacchaeus] too is a son of Abraham. For the Son of Man came to seek out and to save the lost" (Luke 19:9-10).

Liturgy Makes Links

In the classic language of theology we proclaim that God has become a human being, so that every human being can be drawn into God. In terms of the liturgy this truth manifests itself in a practical way. The liturgy is rooted in the ordinariness of the lives we live, so that every moment in those lives can be grasped as a moment of encounter, of discipleship, of grace. Jesus of Nazareth, a specific historical individual whom we confess to be the Word become flesh, went into villages and taught at tables in houses. He entered into the ordinariness of life and there showed us the way to the Father. This is the way of Christian liturgy. Likewise, in liturgy we meet people and meet as people going along our various ways, and these ways become our Way.

Let's take four simple examples that can help to bring out what is meant by incarnational liturgy.

The prayer of the faithful. When Christians gather to worship God and thank God for redemption, we do not forget that we have to ask for the needs of a very messy world full of very urgent and material needs: food, health, and the absence of war. We gather as a bunch of needy people, but we are at the same time the priestly people who stand in the presence of God and make intercession for the everyday needs of ourselves and humanity. We gather in an ordinary space—one can gather anywhere for the Eucharist—and yet we also stand in the court of heaven, making intercession in union with the glorified Christ. It is easy to think of just the ordinariness and our needs. It is easy to think of being a priestly people in the sublime court. This challenge is to keep them together, just as the human and divine natures in the Christ must not be torn asunder.

The table of the Lord. The center of the Christian assembly is the Lord's table: it is our thanksgiving banquet that is the bearer of our greatest memories. For centuries this was hardly visible as such. It was referred to only by the word *altar*, which was a specific interpretation of one aspect of the table. It was far from those who were supposedly gathered around it, and no one noted any link between it and the tables in their homes. There was a gulf between the table of their breakfast (this was the ordinary world of life and living) and the large stone structure in the church (this belonged to "the other" and, indeed, it was understood by how distant it was from everyday life). But Jesus revealed himself when he was elbow to elbow with people at table. It is our everyday understanding of the community of a table that forms the basis for our appreciation of the banquet language of the kingdom. It is the acts of thanks at our daily meals that form the foothills for the summit that is the thanksgiving in Christ at the meal of the church. We have to experience the sense of being gathered around his table, elbow to elbow, if we are to grasp that at every table we may encounter the Word made flesh.

The loaf of the church. For many cultures the basic foodstuff is the loaf of bread, and giving thanks over bread is deep in our memory as the people of God. It is an action that links us to the whole of our story as God's people and is as meaningful today as ever. Most of us are free from the threat of famine, but if we forget our complex links to food, the planet, and others—and being thankful for what sustains us as God's gift—then we have lost the plot as God's creatures. But when we look at the token-sized loaves of altar bread, we could be forgiven for not linking what we eat at the Eucharist with the world of ordinary food. The distinctive part of Jesus' thanksgiving was that he took a loaf, broke it, and shared it; this is what was noteworthy for recording and handing on.[5] But the little individual, precut round wafers are hardly reminiscent of having a piece from a loaf shared with one's sisters and brothers. The logic of the incarnation means that our human experience of sharing at our everyday tables gives us a base to appreciate the sharing in the encounter with God at the eucharistic table. In turn, our sharing at the Eucharist allows us to see the opening to the sacred that is there in every meal and the call of discipleship to be people who share generously with one another,

---

5. Thomas O'Loughlin, "The 'Eucharistic Words of Jesus': An Un-noticed Silence in our Earliest Sources," *Anaphora* 8 (2014): 1–2.

with the poor, the stranger, and the unwanted. To many who see the encounter with Jesus at Mass as so special that it has to be taken out of the world of the ordinary and placed in a separate sacral zone—perhaps hedged off with rails, or screens, or a language far from the everyday—there is this dangerous incarnational memory: "When did we see you hungry and feed you, or . . . a stranger and welcome you, or . . . in prison, and visit you?" (Matt 25:37-39).

The cup of discipleship. One of the few certainties of life is that if you are reading this, you will very shortly drink something! And, when you do, you will almost certainly use a cup of some sort. But it will be *your* cup, and, excepting unusual situations, in any group each person will have his or her own cup. We do not share cups! But the cup of the Lord is *shared,* and it is the sharing that is the feature that was highlighted in the memory.[6] Moreover, there is a link between sharing the cup at the gathering and being willing to share in discipleship and the cross. To each Christian is addressed the question: "Can you drink the cup that I am going to drink?" (Matt 20:22). But the cup of the Lord only makes sense in the depths of our human experience if it is seen both in continuity with every other cup and—in the way that we pass it from one to another—in contrast to them. If the cup is held back for only the presider or a special group, the liturgy does not proclaim that each is called by Jesus—and challenged to take on the fullness of discipleship. Whereas if other solutions are used to avoid sharing the cup (such as dipping, straws, or individual thimbles), we are not

---

6. The little individual prepacked plastic thimbles of wine/grape juice now used by many Reformed churches are as alien to the memory as is the withholding of the cup that is still the default setting among Catholics.

only untrue to the practice of Jesus, but it implies that we think of receiving communion as a sacral commodity, while forgetting that this shared cup stands alongside every other cup we do not share in our lives. Using them, we are struck by the wonder of the Lord's meal while at the same time recognizing that discipleship is not confined to this special cup but is our concern in every situation when we are using cups.

Distinctively Christian

Boundaries between the sacred and the profane—they come in the shape of walls, screens, special languages, a special this or that which makes distinctions—are at the heart of most of the "languages" of human religion. But the created world and the divine world come together in the person of Jesus *and* in the practical realities of the liturgy, and it is in him that we pray and celebrate. In good liturgy the ordinary and the messiness of human existence spill into the beauty and transcendence of the divine *and* wonder and grace of the divine can seep out into every corner of our lives. We need to build bridges rather than boundaries between the so-called ordinary and the so-called sacred. It is this incarnational character of Christian worship that makes it stand apart.

12

Principle X

Good Liturgy Is Open

The heart of the message of Christianity, as of Judaism and Islam, is the infinity of that which we call "God." We express this in any number of theological shorthands: God is one; creation is *ex nihilo*; only God is absolutely generous, or we assert the absolute nonmutuality between Creator and creation. Our liturgy has to convey a sense of this mystery in its style. Doing so is one of the great challenges we face. At the very least we have to make sure that we do not foster false notions that God is some sort of force, "the man upstairs," who is placated or who can be bought. Equally, it means that anything that smacks of meanness, of a narrow and constricted vision, has no place in worship. If God is open and generous, so must our liturgy be!

Trading with God

A god who is one more object within the universe—even if it is an actor of untold power—is not the God of Abraham,

Jesus, or Muhammad. In contrast with this fundamental affirmation of faith is the fact—which seems to be borne out empirically by anthropologists of religions—that most rituals relate to the divine as one more, albeit supreme, force in the universe. Religion then slips into trying to make deals with this god: deals for health, success, protection, and perhaps deals to try to get this god to take one's side in battle or to punish one's enemies. It would be silly to imagine that Christians are somehow immune to this temptation.

It is so easy for our liturgy to drift toward this notion of trading with God; it is little more than the broad range of our human experience. Now our rituals take the shape of "I give it to you so that you might give me something" (*do ut des*). Prayer becomes a petitioning for an audience so as to get influence, a placating as either a down payment (a votive) or a payback (a reparation), or an engaging that seeks to manipulate the processes in the universe. The analysis of this proclivity found in Wisdom 15—assuming you are using the big Septuagint canon for the Old Testament—is as accurate a description of this phenomenon within human religiosity as one can get. It is worth reading it as a reminder of what our liturgy must avoid.

We tend to engage (which of us is immune?) with the divine as another force within a system of forces. Therefore, all Christian liturgy walks a tightrope between asserting our faith in God's interest in us and care for us and performing our rituals in a way that communicates the manipulation of the divine. This is the topic that hardly ever made it into liturgical discussions, but was reserved for the section on the virtue of religion in textbooks of moral theology. There it was conveniently solved by seeing the official liturgy as immune, while popular religion (i.e., that which was outside ecclesiastical law) was prone to superstition. The answer was simple: make everything controlled and all would be well! Alas, it was not, nor is it, that simple.

Fear and Liturgy

Fear is a part of human life: fear of loss, fear for loved ones, fear of failure and illness, fear of matters that threaten us, and fear as an existential reality. And, in all of us, fear and faith interact, and so it is naive to imagine that any human ritual will not have an element of barter, even if we intellectually reject the very notion. A pure *gift love*—to use the language of C. S. Lewis[1]—may be our aim but is inconsistent with our finitude (as we see in the traditional characterization of divine power as mercy toward our infirmities: Wis 15:1). The challenge of liturgy is to give expression to fear and need while not making claims that faith and prayer result in divine favor. While such notions can be dismissed as folk superstition (e.g., chain prayers), popular religiosity (e.g., water from a Marian shrine as a remedy for a sore throat), or the wilder extremes of popular evangelism (e.g., the gospel of blessings), we may find it in a wide range of customs based on what has been called "a piety of counting." In such a piety the emphasis is on the accumulation of pious objects, prayers, visits, donations, or whatever is imagined as a way of attracting divine attention or favor. The opposite to this insidious assumption I call the quality of an "open liturgy" and just as the tendency toward counting, gathering, and imagining that "we have God" is ever present, so must be our sensitivity that God is always greater, and that the liturgy never has a control on the divine: "The wind blows where it wills, and you can hear the sound it makes, but you do

1. C. S. Lewis, *The Four Loves* (London: Collins, 1960).

not know where it comes from or where it goes; so it is with everyone who is born of the Spirit" (John 3:8).

Liturgy and Loyalty Cards

So what would be examples of this quality—or of a conscious attempt to avoid the dangers of a mercantile religion—in liturgy? Here are a few examples.

Catholics have a long tradition of "having Masses said."[2] While there is a strict warning that nothing should be done to give the impression that it is a trading with God, it very quickly slips into the mode of *do ut des*. The mere fact of announcing, "This Mass is being offered for . . ."—often of great importance to those who made the request and gave the stipend—gives the impression of the liturgy as a quantifiable commodity.

In almost every liturgy there is a period of intercessory prayer: the prayer of the faithful being the paradigm example, when the assembly stands and intercedes with the Father as a priestly people. But it is easy to slip into causal language whereby we imagine we can order God to intervene. Likewise, we so easily assume that our will or our side or our view must coincide with the best intentions of the divine will, and our prayer becomes a statement of how we would like the world to be.

Ritual is by its nature repetitive: we know what will happen and past performance is the guide to the future. What was an accident one day becomes significant the next day and is deemed essential the time after that. With this human

---

2. Thomas O'Loughlin, "Treating the 'Private Mass' as Normal: Some Unnoticed Evidence from Adomnáns *De locis sanctis*," *Archiv für Liturgiewissenschaft* 51 (2009): 334–44.

process goes the temptation to imagine that our relationship with God in our worship is dependent on the correct performance of the ritual. Unless the right vestments are used, the correct formulae uttered, the right things done, then nothing happens. But God is ever present, ever loving, and whether one worships on the right mountain or the wrong mountain does not matter, so long as one worships in spirit and in truth (John 4:24).

I am often told that we stopped being hunter-gatherers when farming began in the Fertile Crescent about ten thousand years ago. I always want to add: we may have stopped being hunters, but we became even more obsessive gatherers! Collecting is part of human life—how many loyalty cards have you in your wallet gathering points?—and we bring this tendency into our worship where it can subvert our worship into a consumerism. A period of nine days as a special time of prayer is a good idea—there is the imagined ideal nine days in Acts 1–2 between the Ascension and Pentecost—but what if it becomes the equivalent of collecting all nine? If someone asks, "I missed last Thursday, have I done the novena?" then that person has slipped over into viewing the relationship with God in terms of a commerce with an all-powerful dealer. We Catholics have a long tradition of turning a pastoral blind eye to this sort of thing on the basis that it helps people to pray, but the cost is that we may not help people to grow to the stature to which they are called. We may wonder today at the images of damnation in the visions of St. Margaret Mary Alacoque (1647–90) and find the notion of the Nine First Fridays as an "insurance policy" so that we can get confession before we die as an aberration. But we would be foolish to imagine that the instinct has left our humanity, and it would be even more foolish to imagine that because the churches of the Reformation formally condemned such practices and ridiculed such approaches doctrinally, they are immune from this human foible.

What about minute calculations in liturgy? We might ask such questions as should there be three dollops of water in baptism—or must it be done another way entirely, so many candles for Mass, and was too much water added to the cup? All such questions imagine ritual by analogy to mixing cement on a building-site where the right mix is directly linked to its performance and purpose, or a chemical experiment in which there must be exact quantities. The liturgy, however, is about relationship and story. It is always worth keeping in mind what the *Didache* said in reply to such questions: "If you don't have flowing water, use other water, if not cold water, then use hot!" (7:2). Or indeed what an old priest told a young deacon who was dripping water in milliliters into several cups of wine at the preparation of the gifts: "Listen, sonny, it's a ritual, not a recipe!"

The freedom of the children of God is that a new start is always possible. This is so because God is infinite in openness, mercy, and love. It is this mystery that is the basis for our joy in the liturgy.

13

Conclusion

Why Liturgy Matters

I am often asked why I bother with liturgy. To theologians such concern seems to be a practical distraction from the intellectual matters of weight that could be investigated and discussed. There is often an implicit disdain for the apparently mundane, if not downright childish, issues of how people worship and how that worship relates to the kerygma. Speaking with pastors I often find a similar incomprehension—from the Protestant side this can take an extreme form in the view that liturgy is just a wrapping, perhaps for the children, around the core of listening to the Bible and the preaching, while from the Catholic side there is the still-common extreme: what does it *really* matter, so long as Mass is said! In need of a quick reply I usually follow this line taken from Hans Küng:

> The liturgy is and remains the center of the life of the church. If this can be successfully renewed, won't that also have effects on all the areas of church activity?[1]

1. Hans Küng, *My Struggle for Freedom: Memoirs* (Grand Rapids, MI: Wm. B. Eerdmans, 2003), 285.

However, there is a far more serious reason why good liturgy matters.

We all live our lives with two distinct models of truth. The first concerns matters of our everyday lives, matters of fact, and we experience them very directly with our senses. Is there enough water boiling to make coffee? We know exactly what it means, we know how to check it, and we know that the answer is yes or no. How much does the shopping cost? We will be told exactly at the till, and again it's black and white. What does three times three make? Nine, and any other number is wrong! This model of truth is very important and it is the basis of much of our activity in life; we value it because of its practicality and the way it has built our world. But there is another model without which we would not be human: the truth that concerns us as persons—our feelings, values, poetry and beauty, and, more importantly, relationships, including our relationships with God. Here there are no black/white answers, but rather our statements are attempts to bring our minds into an ever closer relationship with the whole of reality in which each of us is a part. In this latter model, I am always trying to grow in understanding and appreciation of the truth, and it is always more complex. In its fullness I shall experience it only at the end; meanwhile all my statements are approximations, shadows, images, and glimpses.

In every generation there are those who reject one of these two models as no more than a distraction. In our culture there are materialists who believe that life can be grasped with the on/off certainty of a string of digital code, but fail to notice that this will not capture the beauty of the flower though it might fully comprehend its DNA. And there are those who go the other way—a slightly harder task because we all have to face explicit facts like having enough water in the kettle before we try to make coffee—and who think factual knowledge, getting the facts right, is just a terrible bore! But we need both, we live with both, and we need both to live.

These two models of truth rarely overlap: poetry and relationships are in one part of our lives, physics and facts in another. But where they do overlap is in ritual; our liturgy is fully part of the factual world, but it is simultaneously open to mystery. What we do and say and use in liturgy must have authenticity in the world of factual truth, but it must also be open to wonder that is greater than what we see, touch, and taste. If we speak of our joy, then we should seek that that joy be real human joy. Then it has a reality in this world of facts that can speak of the joy of the Lord. If we say that we bless the Father and share the loaf of bread, then when we have an authentic loaf of bread and see what is involved in sharing it, which we taste and touch and see, then we can recall what this means to us who remember (Luke 22:19) the meals of the Christ who is among us, whom we see by faith. When we know what it is to share a cup of wine—oh yes, it is so alien to human culture—then we can start to appreciate drinking the cup that he has to drink (Mark 10:38-39) and will know that this is the cup of discipleship. Liturgy is not only at the center of the Christian life; it stands at the intersection of our two ways of knowing, just as it stands at the intersection between me, an individual, and my belonging to a community. This is why liturgy matters.

Bibliography

Bishops' Committee on the Liturgy. *Music in Catholic Worship*. Washington, DC: US Catholic Conference, 1972.

Bradshaw, Paul F. *Reconstructing Early Christian Worship*. London: S.P.C.K., 2009.

Brody, Hugh. *Maps and Dreams: Indians and the British Columbia Frontier*. Vancouver, BC: Douglas and McIntyre, 1981.

Clark, David. "Order and Chaos in the *Didache*." *Journal of Pentecostal Theology* 25 (2016): 287–96.

Combs-Schilling, M. E. *Sacred Performances: Islam, Sexuality, and Sacrifice*. New York: Columbia University Press, 1989.

Connerton, Paul. *How Societies Remember*. Cambridge: Cambridge University Press, 1989.

Draper, Jonathan A. "Performing the Cosmic Mystery of the Church in the Communities of the Didache." In *The Open Mind: Essays in Honour of Christopher Rowland*, edited by J. Knight and K. Sullivan. London: Continuum, 2015.

Eliade, Mircea. *Myths, Dreams and Mysteries*. London: Harvill Press, 1960. First published as *Mythes, Rêves et Mystères* in 1957.

Küng, Hans. *My Struggle for Freedom: Memoirs*. Grand Rapids, MI: Wm. B. Eerdmans, 2003.

Lewis, C. S. *The Four Loves*. London: Collins, 1960.

Marx, Karl. "The Communism of the Paper *Rheinischer Beobachter*." In *On Religion*, Karl Marx and Friedrich Engels. Moscow: Foreign Languages Publications House, 1957. Essay first published 1847.

McRae, Rachel M. "Eating with Honor: The Corinthian Lord's Supper in the Light of Voluntary Association Meal Practices." *Journal of Biblical Literature* 130 (2011): 165–81.

O'Loughlin, Thomas. "Building Community, Celebrating Liturgy— the continuing challenge." *The Furrow* 67 (2016): 80–91.

———. *The Didache: A Window on the Earliest Christians.* Grand Rapids, MI: Baker Academic, 2010.

———. "Divisions in Christianity: The Contribution of 'Appeals to Antiquity.'" In *Faithful Reading: New Essays in Theology and Philosophy in Honour of Fergus Kerr OP*, edited by S. Oliver, K. Kilby, and T. O'Loughlin, 221–41. London: T&T Clark, 2012.

———. "Eucharistic Celebrations: The Chasm between Idea and Reality." *New Blackfriars* 91 (2010): 423–38.

———. "The 'Eucharistic Words of Jesus': An Un-noticed Silence in our Earliest Sources." *Anaphora* 8 (2014): 12.

———. *The Eucharist: Origins and Contemporary Understandings.* London: Bloomsbury T&T Clark, 2015.

———. "How many priests do we need?" *New Blackfriars* 86 (2005): 642–57.

———. "Introducing a liturgy: Reflecting on a moment of communication." *The Pastoral Review* 11, no. 4 (2015): 4–9.

———. "Sharing Food and Breaking Boundaries: Reading of Acts 10–11:18 as a key to Luke's ecumenical agenda in Acts." *Transformation* 32 (2015): 27–37.

———. "Treating the 'Private Mass' as Normal: Some Unnoticed Evidence from Adomnáns *De locis sanctis*." *Archiv für Liturgiewissenschaft* 51 (2009): 334–44.

———. *Washing Feet: Imitating the Example of Jesus in the Liturgy Today.* Collegeville, MN: Liturgical Press, 2015.

Otto, Rudolf. *The Idea of the Holy.* Oxford: Oxford University Press, 1923. First published in 1917 as *Das Heilige.*

Panek, Jiri. "From Mental Maps to GeoParticipation." *Cartographic Journal* 53 (2016): 300–307.

Penn, Michael. "Performing Family: Ritual Kissing and the Construction of Early Christian Kinship." *Journal of Early Christian Studies* 10, no. 2 (2002): 151–74.

Rothenbuhler, Eric W. *Ritual Communication: From Everyday Conversation to Mediated Ceremony.* Thousand Oaks, CA: Sage, 1998.

Schneiders, Sandra M. "The Foot Washing (John 13:1-20): An Experiment in Hermeneutics." *Catholic Biblical Quarterly* 43 (1981): 76–92.

Susai Raj, Antony. "Dalits at the Eucharistic Table." *Japan Mission Journal* 68, no. 1 (2014): 9–14.

Thibodeau, Timothy M. *William Durand: Rationale IV—On the Mass and Each Action Pertaining to it.* Turnhout: Brepols, 2013.

Turner, Victor. *The Ritual Process: Structure and Anti-Structure.* Hawthorne, NY: Aldine de Gruyter, 1995. First published 1969.

Vogel, Cyrille. "An Alienated Liturgy." *Concilium* 2, no. 8 (1972): 11–25.

Wolter, Michael. "Primitive Christianity as a Feast." In *Feasts and Festivals*, edited by C. Tuckett, 171–82. Leuven: Peeters, 2009.

Woolley, Reginald Maxwell. *The Bread of the Eucharist.* London: A.R. Mowbray, 1913.